E.C.S. No. 694

A CHORAL LEGACY

Edited by Alfred Mann

E. C. SCHIRMER MUSIC COMPANY · 112 SOUTH STREET · BOSTON, MA 02111

E. C. Schirmer Music Company, 112 South Street, Boston, MA 02111
Manufactured in U.S.A.

ISBN 911318-12-7 / E.C.S. Plate No. 2526

for
    The E. C. Schirmer Music Company—
    my colleagues for fifty years—
        Faithfully & gratefully,
            Randall Thompson
Thanksgiving, '74

CONTENTS

Contents

Preface

Shortly before the opening of the Berkshire Music Center at Tanglewood, Serge Koussevitzky, its director, decided that the special occasion called for a special ceremony. The inaugural piece he commissioned, written and presented on the spur of the moment, became a veritable symbol of American choral singing — Randall Thompson's *Alleluia*. Characteristic of the composer's style, the work is at the same time characteristic of a fundamental process in twentieth-century music by which the choral art regained the stage. With the decline of the symphonic ideals of post-Romanticism, choral music rose again to the role of a principal creative medium, and such European names as Kodály, Vaughan Williams, Pepping, and Distler found their American counterparts, represented above all by one name: Randall Thompson.

The chapters of this volume were reprinted from two earlier volumes, which appeared as special issues of the *American Choral Review*.[1] One of these, planned as an offering at the occasion of the composer's seventy-fifth birthday, contained articles by colleagues and friends; the other, issued at the time when Randall Thompson had completed his eightieth year, was a selection of his own essays. The latter, written for the most part as much as twenty years earlier, were newly cast in the form of readings in which the composer presented comments on his texts to David Francis Urrows, his assistant, who acted as compiler of these essays.[2]

---

[1] *The Choral Music of Randall Thompson,* Volume XVI, Number 4 (October, 1974); *Randall Thompson: On Choral Composition,* compiled by David Francis Urrows, Volume XXII, Number 2 (April, 1980).

[2] The comments appear in italic type. The essays were concluded with an article written by the compiler, which also concludes this reprint. The reference to "the present volume" appearing on page 81, and left unchanged in this printing, is therefore to be understood as applying to the original publication of Randall Thompson's essays, *American Choral Review,* Volume XXII, Number 2. The references to Volume XVI, Number 4 contained in this same article were consequently also left unchanged.

Elliot Forbes and James Haar, contributors to the earlier of the two mentioned volumes, were close associates of the composer during the years he served on the faculty of Harvard University, the former being the author of the article on Randall Thompson in the recently published Sixth Edition of *Grove's Dictionary*. The editor was Randall Thompson's assistant while he held the directorship of the Curtis Institute of Music.

A span of more than half a century is covered by the works discussed in these pages. "Randall Thompson has created his own legacy," writes David Francis Urrows, "a legacy that is personal for the sake of sharing his experience with others and that will remain of ineffable quality."

— A.M.

Writing for the Amateur Chorus

A CHANCE AND A CHALLENGE

At the height of the Renaissance, Lorenzo de' Medici wrote a wonderful poem which opens with these words:

Chi non è innamorato
Esca da questo ballo.

It is easy Italian, but a hard couplet to put into English. One might say it meant "Anybody not in love will now please quit the ballroom." Or: "Let anyone who is not lovesick leave the dance floor."

I quote this because, by analogy, if there is anyone here who is not in love with choral music, now is his chance to slip away. If he is not in love with choral singing, let him leave. I am a passionate devotee of choral music. I always have been. But as I set out to tell you what I think and feel about it, I must warn you: I'm on fire about it; and if you don't want to hear what a fanatic has to say on the subject, please go away.

These opening remarks of an address delivered before a meeting of the Intercollegiate Music Council at Yale University in May, 1959, had a curious effect: though written with the best intent, they were frowned upon by some of my distinguished listeners who had doubtless not expected such a tone. The discrepancy of opinion showed that choral music and choral composition had arrived at a crossroads in America, and this phenomenon had arrested my particular interest.

The history of music has taken many turns. Sociological factors, political events, historical incidents, philosophical ideas have changed its course, conditioned its content, brought about its popularity, enlarged its scope, determined its media, opened opera houses, closed churches, closed opera houses, opened churches, silenced — then released — singers, forbidden the intrusion of folk music, then made folk-music a rock on which to build.

It is only today that the latter remark might be construed as a pun. But if so, its truth holds: "Rock" has become one of the many new departures – one that is characteristic of the constant regeneration of music with which I was here concerned.

The ups and downs of music — and of the evolution of music — have been at once more violent and more abrupt than those of any other art. Sometimes it took centuries to effect any change at all; sometimes change was effected overnight. In the United States we have witnessed a mighty change — and a relatively quick one. What has happened in the last hundred years in this country is more rapid than ever happened in the Middle Ages, the Renaissance, or the Baroque. This, of course, has to do with the situation of a young country. But, as Oscar Wilde said, "People have been saying that for 300 years." And of course they are perfectly right.

It is natural that we should not, from the moment Columbus landed, have produced a "school" of musical composition. Columbus didn't stay very long; he didn't come here to teach music.

It is tempting to pause here and reflect for a moment upon what would have happened if Columbus had tried to share with the Noble Savage the art of music of that day – the mysteries of vocal counterpoint. He would have had a hard time, if my own experience in trying to teach the natives five hundred years later is any criterion.

Five hundred years is a long time. We made very little progress for about four hundred of those five hundred years. True, our early singing teachers gave us a modicum of musical literacy; true, there are fine documents of creative strength in early American choral music; true, the Handel and Haydn Society was founded in 1815, only a few years after Haydn's death.

By and large, however, we built our towns and our churches without any serious consideration of the music of Tallis, Byrd, Weelkes, Wilbye, Purcell — or of Monteverdi, Corelli, Vivaldi, Couperin, Rameau, Bach, or Handel. They lived and died without this country paying any attention to them. Thomas Jefferson's musical library extended from works of Purcell's father (also a composer) to Weber's *Der Freischütz*. But Jefferson was an exceptionally cultivated man. It would be unfair to expect many of his compatriots to have had such breadth of musical interest. Throughout the seventeenth, eighteenth and nineteenth century, the level of musical cultivation was extremely low, with only one or two exceptions and only two or three torchbearers.

Our debt to those torchbearers can never be repaid — how they fought and how much of the expansion of music in this country is due to them! I think of Oscar Sonneck, of John Knowles Paine, of Frank Damrosch, whose Oratorio Society at the turn of the century sang his editions of Lassus, Palestrina, Gabrieli. I think of Thomas Whitney Surette and of two outstanding leaders in twentieth-century college choral music: Marshall Bartholomew and Archibald T. Davison.

I could hardly hope to portray the struggle and the enlightened guidance that has brought about the present totally new state of choral music and through it, I believe, of all music in America. The truth is that while many a serious composer has been working in seclusion — doubtless producing fine works — a whole new medium of expression has come into being: nobody ever before had such a medium of communication as composers have today in the amateur chorus.

There are now an immense number of amateur choruses in this country — college and civic choirs, glee clubs and madrigal groups extend across the face of this continent. They have high musical ideals, high musical ambitions. They want to excel: excel in what they sing and in the way they sing it. This is a very special phenomenon of the twentieth century. An immense offering of work and great enthusiasm went into creating it. As a result, here is a new and a truly vast outlet for composers.

Now, composers are very special. They grumble about having no "market"; they grumble about being "unappreciated." Granted, they may be unappreciated. But *not* granted they have no "market." Nothing could be farther from the truth: boys and girls, men and women all across the country and around the world are ready and waiting, eager for new music to perform, fully as eager for it as an Esterházy prince ever was to have a new quartet!

In point of fact, the "outlet" for composers, their "market," is far larger than you and I could possibly estimate with any degree of accuracy. Great though it is, it will be much larger when capable leaders, desperately needed, move into hitherto silent, inert, potentially musical, vocal communities and "unlock their silent throats." This will have to come to pass. There are many more choral groups that want to sing well — and could sing well — than there are good choral conductors to lead them. And the end is not in sight.

Though written twenty years ago, this statement still holds true. The reason is in large part the greatly raised general level of musical education: while a new generation of choral conductors and while professional choruses have come into being, the demand for choral music continues to grow. But a principal reason is the quality of choral music itself. And this is a point that particularly occupied my mind at the time.

What do these people like to sing? Not an antiquated, trite repertory. They want to sing William Byrd, Bach, Beethoven, Berlioz, Brahms. Above all they want to sing more *a cappella* music.

Now there are two things about *a cappella* music. The first is that no chorus can really sing well with an orchestra, or even with piano or organ, until it can sing well by itself without accompaniment. The second is that if a chorus can sing well *a cappella,* a vast body of beautiful music is opened up to it. The whole *a cappella* literature from Dunstable to Monteverdi and extending into the nineteenth and twentieth centuries is the chorus's private domain.

For a long time we did not realize this. Much was done to bring great choral music to our attention, and it did a great deal of good. Men's colleges, taking the lead, sang many hitherto unheard masterpieces. But it was only a step in the right direction, as those responsible for it were the first to say.

I would defend the sensitive "arrangement" of great choral music — the transposition, the change of color and range. I would also defend the good arrangement of folk music — really, for centuries, a subdivision of choral composition. Arrangements can be very useful. But they have their limitations, and they can be carried too far. The chief value of choral arrangements was, and still is, that they enabled choruses of men's voices or of women's voices to enlarge their limited repertories and thus broaden their experience through acquaintance with a great literature. As co-education has spread in this country, the old-fashioned *Männerchor* organizations and ladies' singing societies have become far less common and far less popular.

In a way this is a pity, for there is a fine literature for men's voices and for women's voices alone. It is to be hoped that this literature will never fall into disuse or neglect. The literature for mixed voices is infinitely larger, and greater; and the last hundred years or so have gradually put within easy reach a vast literature of music for mixed voices — sacred and secular — music of infinite variety, music of ineluctable beauty. Whole sets of musical monuments have appeared and are still appearing: English, French, Flemish, German, Spanish, Italian — chansons, madrigals, masses, motets. When I was in college, I procured with some difficulty a handful of Monteverdi's madrigals. Now his whole output is accessible to all. More and more octavo editions appear annually; more and more choral conductors prepare their own working editions. Indeed, I sometimes wonder whether it is co-education that is responsible for the increasing popularity of mixed choruses or whether the beauty of the literature has brought more and more co-educational choruses into being, nourished and sustained them. At any rate, this particular phenomenon — the proliferation of mixed choruses — did not occur, and could not have occurred, a hundred years ago. There would not have been anything to compare with the glory of the presently available literature, either in quality or in extent. Is it too much to say that the literature itself has been the dominant creative and sustaining force in the formation and flourishing of one mixed chorus after another?

Why, under these circumstances, with this unparalleled outlet within easy reach, *why* has there not sprung up in this country a *bona fide* school of choral composers? We hear about the "cultural explosion," but no such "school" has emerged. Of all the many possible reasons for this lack, I am going to select a few and elaborate on each one of them briefly.

1) *The tyranny of the Doctrine of Absolute Music.* This aesthetic fallacy has retarded choral composition in this country more than any other single factor. It has even done harm to the creation of absolute music, because an instrumental style unleavened by the knowledge and experience of writing for voices can become over-instrumental, even turgid, and in effect lose touch with the human spirit. Let me state at once that I consider, for example, Beethoven's C-sharp Minor Quartet one of the greatest achievements in music or, for that matter, in all art. It is, unimpeachably, absolute music. But think how much choral music Beethoven had written before he wrote the C-sharp Minor Quartet. Yet an absolute doctrine of absolute music persists in our day. It does infinite harm to choral music.

It may have been the matter of folk music arrangements, mentioned a little earlier, from which the division of opinion between some members of the audience and myself took its point of departure. But more likely it was this argument of a doctrine of absolute music. Though there was obviously no such intention, it might be applied to the orientation of some of my critics.

2) A second impediment to choral composition is the *difficulty of applying contemporary compositional techniques to writing for chorus.* Modern idioms — the insistence on dissonance and super-chromaticism, on fitful and irregular rhythms; the vogue for intensity and a pervading *martellato* style (so accented throughout that there remains virtually no accentuation at all); the Romantic cultural lag that characterizes many a new work, a total absence of "inner check"; a ranting in tone or an equally excessive quietism — all such stylistic

traits do not lend themselves *a priori* to the medium of the chorus. And as in writing for any medium, so in writing for chorus: it behooves the composer to understand the characteristics, the limitations and the capabilities of his chosen medium.

3) Certain other reasons have worked against the development of choral literature in this country. Writing for voices shows, for instance, quicker than anything else (except perhaps writing for string quartet) the *shortcomings in a composer's technique;* one reason why we have no "school" of choral composers (such as existed, in one period or another, in virtually every European country from the fourteenth through the twentieth century) may be that our young composers haven't acquired sufficient technical equipment. (Of course one never has!)

Meanwhile, many a composer — young and old — has a hard time earning enough to live on. In this I feel real sympathy for them. But my sympathy gives out when they shake their fists at a cruel world and say, "My art is not *wanted;* it is not *appreciated;* there is no *place* for the artist in contemporary civilization." As with Caesar and Brutus, the fault is not in their stars but in themselves. The acts of humility that they must undergo to enter "In diese heil'gen Hallen" may be hard for them to submit to. But it would be wonderful if they would and did.

Let us consider what trials, what tests these young Taminos must undergo.

The first thing that they should realize is this: many of the greatest composers' greatest works are choral, and they can all be sung by amateurs. What would be the good of writing a choral piece that only professionals could sing? If a piece is too difficult for amateurs to sing, the chances are that it is not good enough. It would be a terrible indictment of contemporary schools of composition if, in this respect, they were accused of failing to do what their forebears did so well.

This is probably the hardest statement to maintain in my discussion now that another twenty years have passed. They have brought the developments of the modern professional chorus and of totally new choral idioms inspired by it. Perhaps the best comment I could offer is that these new idioms characterize the problem: they are predominantly developments of the Sprechstimme, *of sounds that the human voice can produce besides singing. The best way to restate my point might be: the farther we move from the natural limitations of the human voice, the farther we move from the nature-given laws of music.*

Writing for voices has been a passionate, life interest of mine. I warned you at the start: I am fanatical on the subject. Would it be decent for me to give you a feather or two out of my own cap?

Above all, choose a good *text* and not too long a text. Don't choose a mawkish, sentimental, obscure, problematic, eccentric text or any text capable of appealing only to a few. Choose a text of some universality, whether serious or comic, sacred or secular. And in choosing it, remember that (as Samuel Johnson said of the ideal prose) you want something "familiar but not coarse, elegant but not ostentatious." There is sometimes a real difference between what is popular and what is great; but there is no difference at all between what is great and what is widely popular over a long period of time.

A few suggestions in connection with your choice of text:

Read and re-read all the poetry you can — try to become a connoisseur of poetry. Do the same thing with prose. There is probably no richer source of beautiful, universal and poetic texts for choral settings than the Bible. A Concordance of the Bible can be enormously helpful in discovering texts.

Having found your text, commit it to memory. Sing it to yourself in a thousand different ways. Decide on the best, the most fitting melody for it. Don't worry about progressions; let the tune and the words determine the form. Let the music follow the *rhetoric* of your texts. Don't set a question in the text with a full cadence in the tonic. Don't place subordinate clauses in the very heart of the central tonality. Above all, place the voices where they will *sound*. Avoid inappropriate chromaticism. Avoid extreme ranges. Avoid unnecessary *divisi* in the individual parts. And finally sing the individual parts to yourself. If you *can* sing them, it doesn't necessarily mean that they are good; but if you *can't* sing them, there's something wrong, and you had better do some serious re-touching.

I have found it useful not only to search carefully for texts, but also to keep a file of poems or prose that might some day come in handy. My "file" has stood me in good stead. Years before I set it to music, I happened on the text of "The Last Words of David" in a Gideon Bible in a hotel room. When subsequently Koussevitsky asked me — at the point of a gun — to write a short choral piece for a documentary film on Tanglewood, I had the text in hand — and the gun never went off.

The first lines — the ones that set my mind to work — for a more recent large work written for a double chorus I happened to see on the front page of the *London Times*. In 1953 I wrote a little choral tribute *(Felices Ter)* to Dr. Davison on his seventieth birthday: the text was an inscription on a gate leading into Harvard Yard.

Don't worry about so-called ugly sounds in a text: difficult vowels or clusters of consonants, e.g., "make his paths straight." A good conductor will overcome any such difficulty. Just as there is, in the absolute sense, no "ugly" color, no "ugly" chord, so there is, in the absolute sense, no "ugly" combination of vowels or consonants.

Don't believe for a moment that, to be good, the musical setting must follow slavishly the natural declamation of the words. Naturally, one does not miscalculate words or syllables, except for very special effects; and naturally one does not stress unimportant words, especially prepositions. But neither does one have to follow the exact rhythm of the spoken word. Plainsong, noted for its natural declamation, is not always faithful to the normal accentuation of the text. But whether or not it is basically declamatory, it is supremely beautiful monophony. It has been said that Palestrina is a kind of polyphonic plainsong. This simply is not so. Here is a Palestrina phrase, a setting (chosen at random) of the word "Benedictus":

EXAMPLE 1

be - ne - dic - - - - - - - - - - - tus

The beauty of the line makes us think nothing at all of the incongruity of the duration of the "*i*" in "Benedictus." But to return to our point, it is the syllable with the *tonic accent* that receives the melisma. This is good, though it cannot be made into a rule. Both plainsong and the polyphony of the Palestrina style place melismas on unaccented syllables. The most conspicuous example of this practice is the traditional *jubilus* at the end of the word "alleluja." But it works better with the final *a* than with most final unaccented syllables in English. We do not like to sing "beautifu-u-u-l." Above all, no one likes to sing a melisma on the inflected final syllable of a verb, e.g., "gaz-i-i-ing." This obscures the beauty and meaning of the word and accentuates instead the participial ending common to all verbs in the English language! No aspect of choral composition is harder to teach or to be specific about than choral prosody. There are virtually no hard-and-fast rules. The best way to acquire an instinctive feeling for it is to read poetry well and thoughtfully and, above all, to read it aloud. This is why it is a good idea to commit one's text to memory before starting to set it to music.

I have dwelt at some length on this point because composers are apt to be over-timid about "texting." or finicky, or careless. Ideally the music seems to grow out of the words. Certainly it must not be sacrificed to them. Music was never sacrificed to the words in Schubert's songs. How simple the problem can be is shown best of all in a traditional *ballad*. There the same music takes care of perhaps thirty verses or more.

Some strange prosody crops up in the stanzas of our hymns. On the other hand, consider the strophic ayres of Dowland or Ford, or the strophic choruses of Mendelssohn or Brahms. In "Marias Kirchgang" from the *Marienlieder*, Brahms used the same music for five or six stanzas; for one other he wrote special music, not because the prosody required it, but in order to suggest the church bells that, according to the legend, rang out miraculously.

The best rule remains: sing the words to yourself. If the melody brings out the feeling of the text and the significance of the important words and of the important syllables, then the prosody is good — then the musical rhythm and the rhythm of the poetry or prose are blended to create the rhythmic ebb and flow of the choral parts.

Some final technical observations:

In many contemporary works the time-signature changes every bar or so. This particular mannerism works rather badly with voices, especially with unaccompanied voices. Rather than differentiating rhythm, it distorts rhythm, and undistorted rhythm, whether slow or fast, is the singer's most important aid. Of course, occasional changes of meter are unavoidable. But constant or capricious changes (that perhaps just a fermata or an accent would render superfluous) make singers uncomfortable. The attacks become shaky; pitch suffers. Meanwhile, perhaps the whole passage could have been written in 4/4 time in the first place.

Repetition of words can be rhetorically highly effective: "Gloria! Gloria! Gloria!" or "Gone! Gone! Gone!". But "Full many a glorious morning have I seen, I seen" doesn't make sense to either singers or listeners. Words in any given line should never become meaningless fragments.

Be sure to check your syllabification by consulting a dictionary. Your editor may do it for you — or he may not. We sing "ligh-ting," but it must be printed "light-ing" (a very common type of error even in published music).

My last suggestion: I want to emphasize the great importance of learning to write well for unaccompanied chorus before trying to write accompanied works. Just as a chorus that cannot sing well *a cappella* cannot sing well with piano or orchestra, so a composer who cannot write well for *a cappella* chorus cannot hope to write really well for accompanied chorus.

In re-reading this passage, I am struck by the realization that more than three-hundred years ago Heinrich Schütz gave similar advice to the young composer of his day (Preface for the Geistliche Chormusik, *1648). He called on the principles of the Renaissance to stem the tide of the Baroque. But such "Rebirth" will go through the ages as long as there are new generations of young composers.*

*   *   *

What, we might ask in the end, are the immediate advantages, what are the rewards of writing for chorus, men's, women's, mixed?

To cite perhaps the most direct advantage first: choral compositions can be an asset to a composer. At the beginning of his career, his *orchestral* works are often liabilities to him under our present musical economy. On the other hand, a good list of well-written choral works with good texts can supplement his annual income and perhaps enable him to keep on writing.

But far more important will remain the purifying and refining effect that writing for chorus will have on his musical style, both choral and instrumental. The individual parts of a choral piece must have character and interest if the singers are to be moved in any way by it; if they are not moved, they will not perform it well, their hearers will be apathetic, and the piece a failure. In order to succeed, a choral composer has to make his emotional intent crystal clear. A kind of fundamental simplicity is blessedly imposed upon him. But this should not make him feel constricted or thrown into chains. Fundamental simplicity is one of the outstanding characteristics of good music, of good art. To learn to be simple never did any artist any harm. True, the line between simplicity and banality is often only a thread. That pitfall obviously has to be avoided. But a composer who cannot do a simple thing well cannot be relied upon to do a complex thing well. Writing for voices may refine a potentially turgid style.

What gives me the greatest joy and the deepest inner satisfaction, and what I regard as the highest reward of all, is to know that the choral music I write is sung by boys and girls, men and women who are amateurs — and it is well to remember that the original meaning of the word is entirely positive. I put the notes on paper: they sing it;

they are doing something they love to do, just as I have been.

Naturally a composer is pleased to have a Symphony Hall or a BBC performance of an orchestral work. But one can be just as much pleased by performances of a choral work of small choirs, choruses, glee clubs. One is pleased, too, and strangely affected when one hears that one's work has been sung by high-school students or by the choir of a little church in Kentucky, or by a naval college in Japan, a group of students in Korea, or a Hindu "Madrigal Society" in Bombay. Those are things that make one realize what writing music really means and what responsibility it carries with it; those are the things that make financial profit seem a very minor consideration; those are the things that lift up one's heart, that give one the courage to go on, the incentive to try and make it better the next time.

Haydn summed the whole matter up when he heard that *The Creation* had been performed on a small island in the Baltic Sea. From the little town of Bergen, capital of the island of Rügen in the Baltic, a society of amateurs wrote to thank him for the pleasure that performing his *Creation* had given its membership. Haydn replied:

> Gentlemen:
>
> It was a truly agreeable surprise to me to receive so flattering a letter from a quarter to which I could never have presumed that the productions of my feeble talent would penetrate. Not only do you know my name, I perceive, but you perform my works, fulfilling in this way the wish nearest my heart: that every nation familiar with my music should adjudge me a not wholly unworthy priest of that sacred art. On this score you appear to quiet me, so far as your country is concerned; what is more, you give me the welcome assurance — and this is the greatest comfort of my declining years — that I am often the source from which you, and many other families receptive to heartfelt emotion, derive pleasure and satisfaction in the quiet of your homes. How soothing this reflection is to me!
>
> Often, as I struggled with obstacles of all kinds opposed to my works — often, as my physical and mental powers sank, and I had difficulty in keeping to my chosen course — an inner voice whispered to me: "There are so few happy and contented men here below — on every hand care and sorrow pursue them — perhaps your work may some day be a source from which men laden with anxieties and burdened with affairs may derive a few moments of rest and refreshment." This, then, was a powerful motive to persevere, this the reason why I can even now look back with profound satisfaction on what I have accomplished in my art through uninterrupted effort and application over a long succession of years.[1]

---

[1] Quoted from Oliver Strunk, "Haydn," in David Ewen, ed., *From Bach to Stravinsky* (New York: W.W. Norton, 1933), p. 85.

On Contrapuntal Technique

Asked to speak about "Modal Counterpoint in the Liberal Arts Curriculum" at the Third Annual Meeting of The College Music Association in Cleveland, Ohio, in 1950, I reflected on what was then a span of about twenty-five years of teaching counterpoint and confessed:

My heart still leaps up when I see a cantus firmus. I do not say that I would rather write exercises than music. But I do say that, when I find myself alone of an evening, I would far rather try my hand at triple counterpoint or the solution of a puzzle canon than at solving a crossword puzzle or reading a detective story. In fact, I will tell you (confidentially) that for more than ten years I have been working this way, in off hours, trying to solve the puzzle canon that serves as colophon to the first volume of Padre Martini's *Esemplare* and the canon that Neukomm wrote for Haydn's epitaph. So far I have made no progress at all, for all my hours of loving labor. If any of you know how to solve either one of them, I should be glad to hear of it; but please do not tell me what the solution is: I want to solve at least one of them by myself. I like to think that I may, still, get to heaven with a solution in my hand.

At the close of the meeting, Hans T. David, the Bach scholar, who happened to be a member of the audience, kindly explained to me one reason for the difficulty I had experienced: The canon that Sigismund Ritter von Neukomm, Haydn's devoted friend and student, had written for Haydn's tomb, using Haydn's favorite Horace text non omnis moriar ("I shall not wholly die") was incorrectly reproduced in Grove, which had served as my source. The trouble was mended years later, for the article on Neukomm contained in Die Musik in Geschichte und Gegenwart *is accompanied by a handsome facsimile reproduction of the composer's autograph (Table I). But meanwhile I had written to Karl Geiringer, author of the well-known Haydn biography, to whom I am greatly obliged – not only did he answer by sending me an accurate copy of the canon, but he added his own ingenious solution (Ex. 2). Thus the task I had set for myself was narrowed down to work (as yet not completed!) on Martini's canon (Table II).*

Table I: The inscription on the right side of the manuscript reads: "Canon for Jos. Haydn's tomb from his pupil S. Neukomm." Above the upper line of music appears the inscription *Five-part Riddle Canon*, and above the lower line is written: "*N.B.* This canon must be notated in the following manner before a solution is attempted."

EXAMPLE 2:

The entire text of my paper on "Modal Counterpoint in the Liberal Arts Curriculum" would stray too far from the interest of this journal's readers. But the comments inspired at that occasion by the figure of Padre Martini and by the didactic method of this great guardian of vocal polyphony – J.C. Bach's and Mozart's teacher – might well be retained in the present context:

The examples, and the commentary on them, are the chief glory of Padre Martini's *Esemplare* — his "Fundamental and Practical Essay on Counterpoint" (Bologna, 1774/75). This famous work gives only ten rules for counterpoint because to give more would necessitate so many exceptions that it is better to study the exceptions (says Padre Martini) as they occur in actual music. It is certainly the most valuable adjunct to the teaching of Modal Counterpoint. To cite just one example, let me call your attention to one of the fifty or sixty complete musical illustrations that serve as the basis for the first volume of the work. He reproduces in full Palestrina's *Quae vox quae poterit,* a motet in the Phrygian mode; and in his running commentary he prints the plainsong melody on which it is based. The music, in conjunction with the plainsong melody, is indeed a graceful, elevating example of Palestrina's chief method of composition. The liberal

256

gli Antichi, oggi giorno vengono proibiti 121.

Vocali lunghe proferite brevi, e le brevi proferite lunghe, difetto ne' Compofitori, e ne' Cantanti, non folo Antichi, ma ancora Moderni 121.

Willaert (Adriano) Maeftro del Zarlino, e del P. Porta 165. lodato dal Zarlino 212.

Z

Zarlino (Giofeffo), vedi Principio Armonico, di lui opinione intorno l'Antifona *Nos qui vivimus* 202.

Vidit

Table II: Final page from Giambattista Martini, *Esemplare o sia saggio fondamentale prattico di contrappunto*, Volume I, Bologna, 1774.

quality of Martini's teaching has always appealed to me, and I find Fux's *Gradus ad Parnassum* equally rewarding from the teacher's point of view. The great thing about Martini and Fux, it seems to me, is the particular *tone* of their teaching. And this brings me to the special problem of the *teacher* of Modal Counterpoint.

For the teacher, I can think of no better ideal than the attitude of kindly interest and encouragement that is exemplified by Fux and Martini. In dealing with so difficult a subject, kindness, patience and helpfulness are essential — and the only road to success. A student who does good work must constantly be led to attempt more. A student in difficulty must constantly be helped to an understanding of first principles. No amount of time and patience, constructive effort, and positive encouragement can be spared, if the work is to go forward.

A teacher of Modal Counterpoint should recognize the importance of working solutions at the blackboard and be capable of it. (Thinking out loud as he works at the board is one of the most constructive pedagogical methods that I know of.) He should be capable of admitting any exceptions to the "rules," and admitting them cheerfully, provided anything can be found in Palestrina which justifies such exceptions. And if there is nothing in Palestrina to justify breaking the established rules, even then he can sometimes let a violation pass — if it seems musically warranted — and thereby win more loyalty to the rules of the game than he ever would by being a Beckmesser.

He should, in fact, be able not only to write exercises at the blackboard, but also to compose a motet at the board — again thinking out loud and conferring with the class as to the advantages of doing this or that. Of course, one takes one's life into one's hands — but when it goes well, it can be very stimulating to both teacher and class. I once wrote a motet at the board for some students of mine (see pages 26-27). It all began because they voiced a complaint about having to use Latin texts. I explained to them that the use of Latin texts was one of the real advantages in studying the contrapuntal art of the sixteenth century; but, at the same time, I saw no reason to insist. So I used a text that they could all obviously understand and added an *Alleluia* as a closing phrase. Naturally they were all familiar with that word — though I confess I did not venture to ask them what it meant. After this, I had that particular class set English texts for a while. In the end, they rather took pride in setting Latin.

This brings me to the point where I should like to say a few special words about the Modal Counterpoint *student*. I shall confine myself to some maxims.

Somewhere in the *Ars Poetica* Horace says: *Non satis est pulchra esse poemata.* "Beautiful versification is not enough." A student should remember that mere "correctness," mere freedom from errors, is not enough. And in another famous line in the same poem Horace says as much, once and for all: *In vitium ducit culpae fuga, si caret arte.* "The avoidance of error can lead to wrong, when there is a lack of art." Let the student remember that any study of theory worthy of the name is basically a study of the art of musical composition. The freedom involved is only a matter of degree. At times, even, a composer is far less free than the student who is trying to solve a theoretical problem: because a composer, by his own hands, can create a problem that he has to solve, which is of a difficulty undreamt of in any purely academic exercise.

Two other maxims are good for the student to call to mind. Donald Tovey says in his *Encyclopedia Britannica* article on Counterpoint: "What is always important is the peculiar life breathed into harmony by contrapuntal organization." The full realization of the truth of this can come to the student only long after his contrapuntal studies are behind him. But the knowledge of it should serve at least to give an added impulse and direction to his efforts.

The last maxim that I shall cite for the student is from Fux's *Gradus ad Parnassum.* Aloysius (who represents Palestrina) is speaking, and he compliments Joseph (who represents the author) on the rightness of a certain solution to a musical problem. He says: "That is very observant and thoughtful, because *one should equally consider ease of singing and correctness of progressions.*" (Italics mine.) The student of Modal Counterpoint is, when all is said and done, studying the art of choral composition, and he will do well to remember it. He is learning how to write for voices, because the whole art of the Polyphonic Period and all that it bespeaks — its technique, its expression, its evolution, its perfection; every rule, every point of practice — all were determined by a single practical and aesthetic standard of what was singable, most natural, most beautiful, and most appropriate to the art of choral music.

Now I lay me down to sleep

R.T. (in class)
May 8, 1947

The Story of an *Alleluia*

In contemplating the account given of my luck at puzzle canons, it occurred to me that I may lay claim to solving one particular puzzle that had long escaped solution. Since the work on this one also offers new reflections on the question of arrangements touched upon in the first of these essays, the following report might serve a double purpose.

Late in the spring of 1940, Dr. M.A. DeWolfe Howe, as Chairman of the Board of Trustees of the Boston Symphony Orchestra, wrote asking me to compose a choral work in celebration of the opening of the Berkshire Music Center. It had long been Dr. Koussevitzky's dream to form such an institution. He had asked me for a fanfare to celebrate the event. I accepted the commission, but in view of the state of Europe and the Fall of France at that time, I could write no fanfare. Instead, *Alleluia* was written in fulfillment of Dr. Koussevitzky's request.

Alleluia was composed (July 1-5, 1940) for four-part chorus of mixed voices and was first performed after a single rehearsal at Tanglewood, by the entire student body, conducted by Professor G. Wallace Woodworth on July 8, 1940. It was soon performed by other choruses in America and abroad. Later I was urged to write arrangements for men's voices alone and also for soprano and alto alone.

It has always been my intention to write for a specific group of voices which seemed particularly appropriate to the terms of the request, and not to write for them in a complicated or difficult medium. Certain types of choral combinations seem particularly appropriate to certain choirs or combinations of voices. Complex substitutions of parts often seem strangely inappropriate, and the substitution of irrelevant harmonic arrangements, which often omit intended progressions, are clearly out of place.

For several years, therefore, it seemed undesirable to transcribe *Alleluia* for any combination of voices other than four-part mixed chorus. Meanwhile, however, I received various proffered arrangements, none of which, for one reason or another, proved acceptable. The truth is, no possible arrangement of the work seemed in any way satisfactory to me. When transposed, the range of voices was impractical, and the balance of voices, when altered, in no way reflected the original intent. For two reasons, therefore, I was tempted to abandon the whole idea: no arrangement for men's or women's voices alone was singable, and no arrangement followed the spirit or letter of the original score. Before doing so, however, I wrote to my teacher, colleague, and friend, Dr. Archibald T. Davison, a past master in making choral arrangements. I thought to myself that he, if anyone, could help me, but his reply only bore out my conviction. I quote from his charming letter:

Brant Rock, Massachusetts
April 17, 1957

Dear Randall:

    I really wonder if my arranger's hand, so long idle, has not lost whatever cunning it once had. Perhaps because I know it so well the *Alleluia* balks me at every turn when I try to cast it for men's voices. I had most success with it when I preserved the original key but in the end it comes out an entirely different piece and too obviously an arrangement. The need for constant inversion of the voices, reduction of the number of parts, etc., produces too serious a distortion of the original. A parallel case is Holst's Swansea Town which he or someone arranged for men's voices. When performed it comes out no more than a parody of the original. With the *Alleluia* I have tried everything that my poor ingenuity could suggest but to no avail! One difficulty is that as it stands it just defies you to tamper with it. If any men's voice society wants to go it on their own terms, I would say quite firmly, "Gentlemen, shall we join the ladies?"

Always devotedly,
Doc.

To this I could only reply:

Cambridge, Massachusetts
April 19, 1957

Dear Doc:

    I cannot thank you enough for looking over *Alleluia* with regard to casting it for men's voices. In a way I am glad that you find it impossible to do so. This restores my faith in myself, for I have tried repeatedly and failed to find any acceptable solution, and I know that if you cannot find one it simply can't be found.

Gratefully,
Randall

Here the case rested. Dr. Davison lived until 1961, and it was not until eleven years after our exchange that any new light was shed on the problem of arranging *Alleluia*. In the spring of 1968 — twenty-eight years after the piece was written — while I was working in my study and pondering about the unsolved problem, an acceptable solution suddenly came to my mind. My excitement would be hard to describe: I suddenly realized that many of the passages in *Alleluia* had been written, unintentionally, in four-part invertible counterpoint. The voices that would have to be literally transposed from the original, whether for men's or women's voices, and which yielded a tessitura too high or too low, proved readily invertible, in one way or another. Note by note, the inversion of the voices could be chosen to preserve the original melodies and harmonies.

The reader will notice that this is not the usual design prescribed by the technique of quadruple counterpoint, such as one finds in the fugues of the *Well-Tempered Clavier* of J.S. Bach, where the same material appears in a succession of inversions.[1]

In recasting the harmonies of *Alleluia* to cover new tessituras, parts are inverted here and there for the convenience of the singers. Inversions do occur in *Alleluia*, but not with fugal consistency. A specific example of total choral inversion appears in measures 20-22, where the original SATB becomes TBAS. A complete listing of inversions is shown in Table III.

I should add here a mention of one adjustment included in the printed edition of the transcription – an adjustment consisting of a single note. In measure 67 of the original version the tenor part appears alone on the first beat, the other voices entering after an eighth rest. In the transcribed version of this passage the tenor assumes the original alto part, yet, rather than beginning the measure with an eighth rest, sings an eighth note doubling the lone opening sound (which in the inverted arrangement might otherwise be too weak). But even here one could say that the contrapuntal inversion remains strict: it is simply applied one eighth note later to this part than to the others.

Of course, not all music is invertible. In reference to our present solution to the problem, some may readily say that the solution was obvious, and had been so all along. The length of time that elapsed before anyone arrived at it suggests that it was not altogether easy. It was a little like Columbus and the egg! When music *does* invert well, the use of inversions can set forth the passages concerned with logic and unity.

My thoughts revert to Dr. Davison with regret that he never knew the published versions of *Alleluia* for men's and for women's voices alone. I cannot conclude without acknowledging my debt to him. It is perhaps enough to say that the form and nature of this work and its arrangements can be attributed, in large measure, to his inspired teaching and profound musicianship.

[1] See, for example, Walter Piston, *Counterpoint* (New York: W.W. Norton, 1947), pp. 182, 183.

Table III: Inversions and their Locations

Upper case letters A B C D represent the order of vocal parts as they appear in the original. Lower case letters show the inversions required for the convenience of tessitura. The same inversions are used in the arrangements for women's and men's voices, the version for women's voices simply being an octave higher than that for men's voices. Of the numerous possible inversions, five are used:

	1	2	3	4	5
	a	c	a	c	a
	c	d	d	a	b
	b	b	b	b	d
	d	a	c	d	c

Measures	1-6	7-11	12-19	20-21	22	23-30	31	32-36	37-41	42-54	55-58	59-64	65-66	67-68	69-78
A	A	a	A	c	c	a	c	a	A	a	a	a	A	a	A
B	B	c	B	d	a	c	a	c	B	c	d	b	B	c	B
C	C	b	C	b	b	b	b	b	C	b	b	d	C	b	C
D	D	d	D	a	d	d	d	d	D	d	c	c	D	d	D

Notes on a *Requiem*

The work was commissioned on February 23, 1957 by the University of California for the dedication of its new music buildings. Scored for double chorus of mixed voices, unaccompanied, it was composed in Cambridge, Massachusetts, from November 20, 1957 to March 21, 1958, on a text drawn from the Holy Bible by the composer. It was first performed as part of the May T. Morrison Music Festival by the University of California Chorus under the direction of Professor Edward Lawton—the chorus and conductor to whom the work is inscribed—at the dedication of the Alfred Hertz Memorial Hall of Music, Berkeley, California, on May 22 and 23, 1958. A recording (limited edition) was made from a concert performance by the Harvard Glee Club and the Radcliffe Choral Society, Professor Elliot Forbes, conductor, at the Sanders Theatre, Harvard University, on April 24, 1959, and the score was published in 1963 by E. C. Schirmer Music Company, Boston, Massachusetts (243 pp.). Certain parts and individual choruses were later published separately, and a complete octavo edition was issued in 1974. The work is not a liturgical Mass. It is a Requiem cast in the form of a dramatic dialogue between two choruses, depicting the triumph of faith over death. Performing time: about an hour and a quarter, with one-minute pauses between the various parts. In view of the length of the *Requiem*, appropriate excerpts from it would have been too copious to include here. Instead, parts of the essay are designed to be read with the music at hand. Page and measure numbers refer to the published score.

Background

The idea of writing a Requiem first came to me in the summer of 1954. On the front page of the London *Times* an *In Memoriam* quoted Psalm 21:4 from The Book of Common Prayer: "He asked life of Thee and Thou gavest him a long life: even for ever and ever." I had been looking for an elegiac text. I cut out the passage and put it in my pocket.

Soon afterwards, again in an issue of *The Times*, I read another biblical quotation: "Can I hear any more the voice of singing men and singing women?" (II Samuel 19:35). This passage, which later became the central dramatic climax of the work, I likewise cut out and put in my pocket.

These two quotations from the Old Testament led to thinking about the possibility of a dramatic work, for unaccompanied chorus, about life and death. Obviously, if it was to be dramatic, there must be conflict. Since one choir alone could hardly convey the idea of conflict, I began thinking in terms of a double chorus, two forces in conflict with each other. Then, too, if there was to be conflict, there must also be its resolution: the catharsis—the emotional cleansing and elevation so essential, esthetically, to the fulfillment of a tragic theme. And what medium more sublime than the double chorus for exaltation and the affirmation of faith?

At first I looked no further for texts: the drama itself was the important thing. Slowly it formed itself in my mind as being in five parts, in some ways not unlike the five acts of Elizabethan tragedy; and it would be cast in the form of a dramatic dialogue between the two choruses, one representing souls of the faithful; the other, mourners. I thought: Part I, *Lamentations*. The mourners grieve and no efforts of the faithful can console them. Part II, *The Triumph of Faith*. A debate on immortality, won in the end by the faithful through a mystic demonstration of eternal life. Part III, *The Call to Song*. With increasing intensity, the souls beseech the mourners to cast off grief through praising the Lord. Finally, in response to the souls' anguished cry, "Can I hear any more the voice of singing men and singing women?", the mourners break forth into song. Part IV, *The Garment of Praise*. A cumulative paean. Part V, *The Leave-taking*. The souls return to their rest and the mourners, all passion spent, submit to God's will and grieve no more the loss of their loved one. "He asked life of Thee and Thou gavest him a long life, even for ever and ever."

It was a happy coincidence when Professor David Boyden of the University of California asked me to write a work for the University Chorus that I had founded (1937): for I was waiting for a chance to write just such a work. Early in October, 1957, on sabbatical leave, I set about putting the synopsis into the form of a dramatic dialogue built out of passages from the Scripture. In one Book or another, the Bible says everything that one could wish to say in a sacred text and says it in the most beautiful way. With the aid of a biblical concordance, I was able to track down an abundance of passages relevant to the dramatic situations in the synopsis by looking under key words such as *mourn, cease, consumed, sing, joy, praise, return*. As it was discovered, each passage was written out on a small card: green cards for one chorus, white cards for the other. To avoid undue length, only the finest and most pertinent passages were retained. These were then arranged in logical sequence to form the dialogue. In the end, the text was compiled from seventeen different Books of the Bible: twelve from the Old Testament, one from the Apocrypha, and four from the New Testament. After six weeks devoted entirely to the preparation of the text, the musical setting was begun.

Double Chorus and Choral Sequence

Of all choral media, the double chorus of mixed voices is perhaps the richest in resources. The very sound of it can hardly fail to impress the listener with its inherent dignity, its serenity, its potential grandeur. This explains, at least in part, why the double chorus was so frequently employed in the Golden Age of Polyphony, and has been ever since, for expressions of exalted, even sublime, subjects. Apart from the fullness and beauty of its sonority in tutti passages, the double chorus (SSAATTBB) offers numerous special advantages:

1. It automatically extends up and down, the comfortable range of all the parts as compared with four-part writing. The first chord in the example below is what might be called risky; the second is wholly practical.

EXAMPLE 1

2. Singers must breathe and, therefore, without a certain art, four-part choral writing loses its legato. (Many devices of counterpoint owe their origin to the wish on the part of composers to conceal this quite understandable shortcoming in human beings.) Two choruses can readily overlap, producing a constant flow of sound, even in chordal passages, as legato as the organ.

3. The double chorus yields an almost inexhaustible variety of color combinations: men's versus women's voices, altos and basses versus sopranos and tenors, etc. In polyphonic, not chordal, eight-part writing the colors shift and change prismatically, like the colors of wind, brass, strings, and their combinations in an orchestra.

4. Occasional lapses into seven (or less) independent parts can permit reinforcement of a given line, either in unison or at the octave. The predominance of such a reinforced line will result automatically

by virtue of the *divisi* (e.g., Soprano I and Soprano II) in the other voices. Such doubling may be of two kinds as, for example, Alto I and II, or Alto II and Tenor I, or Tenor II and Bass I in unison.

5. Last, but not least, the double chorus can greatly increase the endurance of the singers through the alternation of the many inherently available four-part choruses, whether mixed, or men's and women's, or other contrasting pairs of four-part choruses, such as SSTT and AABB, that may be formed within the double-chorus medium. In extended forms and works of a large scale for unaccompanied chorus this is an important consideration; for when the singers' endurance is overtaxed, the whole interpretation of the work—not to mention pitch—is liable to suffer. Regarding the *Requiem*, therefore, the choice of double chorus was indicated not only by the dialogue form of the text but also by its length. This is an example of the influence of text and subject matter on the choice of medium. The text could, supposedly, have been set for four-part chorus, but it is doubtful that any such chorus could have weathered a performance of it.

In drawing up choral programs, I have long felt the need for groups of works which are somehow related to each other, to avoid a patchwork of isolated, heterogeneous works, however excellent in themselves. Such groups, or sequences, or cycles, of choruses can be of three general kinds, with some possible overlapping: 1. those based on a unifying idea (the writer's *Americana*); 2. those drawn from the texts of a single author (*Odes of Horace*; *Rosemary*; *The Testament of Freedom*; *Ode to the Virginian Voyage*; *Frostiana*); and those based on the unfolding of a dramatic narrative (*The Peaceable Kingdom*; *Mass of the Holy Spirit*—the text of the Mass being, in the words of the late Professor Karl Young of Yale, the greatest drama ever written).

The *Requiem* is an extension of the idea that prompted the writing of *The Peaceable Kingdom*. At the American Academy in Rome (1922–25), I heard beautiful performances of the madrigal sequences of Vecchi and Banchieri. Here was drama; here was unity of idea expressed through a succession of madrigals. Why not apply such means to the writing of a *sacred* work? True, the Polyphonic Period produced many series of motets, hymns, and spiritual madrigals (such as Palestrina's to the Virgin and his settings from the *Song of Songs*) but such things did not entail dramatic narrative. In fact, the use of the unaccompanied chorus for sacred drama seems to have been rare indeed. One might cite Willaert's *Susannah*, but it would be hard to name many more such works. The liturgy did not call for them, and obviously left little room for music of a non-liturgical character. Even Monteverdi, whose madrigal sequences are highly dramatic, did not apply the technique to a sacred theme.

The *Requiem* goes somewhat further than *The Peaceable Kingdom* in religious drama-like treatment of the double chorus. In the latter, the two choruses always sing as one: in the *Requiem* they represent opposing forces, individually personified throughout the work. Such personification, too, has its roots in music of the Renaissance, which abounds in secular dialogues between two choruses such as Lassus's exquisite *Que dictes tu* (a conversation between a love-sick one and a turtledove) and his *Zanni* (a little *Commedia dell'Arte scena* between Pantalon and his manservant). Here again, however, such a disposition of choral forces conversing with each other seems not to have been employed in *sacred* music of the Polyphonic Period. This is what I attempted to do, both in *The Peaceable Kingdom* and in the *Requiem*.

Some Technical Considerations

Certain technical problems inevitably arise in composing an extended *a cappella* work for double chorus:

1. *Equality of the two choruses.* This is important, for obvious reasons. One would not wish to overtax one chorus and slight the other. Neither would it be advisable to make the music of one more inviting than that of the other, lest one chorus be crowded with singers, and recruits for the other hard to find. This problem was solved at least in part during the preparation of the text of the *Requiem*, but a certain equality still had to be borne in mind while writing the music. When the text called for *cori spezzati* (e.g., "What man is he," pp. 45–69), the problem did not exist. Nor did it exist when both choruses joined on an equal footing in a single movement (e.g., most of Part IV, *The Garment of Praise*, and "Walk as children of light," Part V, pp. 187–208). The problem was present when it came to distributing equitably the separate sections for Chorus I alone and those for Chorus II alone. There are, by rough count, six such sections for Chorus I and four for Chorus II. This inequality, however, is counterbalanced by the greater share which Chorus II has in the first and last movements of the work. Another instance of a concern for parity is that the work contains three fugues: one for Chorus I, one for Chorus II, and one in which both participate. Still another is the opening section of Part V, "Ye were sometimes darkness," which is given out by Chorus I and repeated a tone higher by Chorus II. When extreme ranges were called for, Chorus I was generally but not always regarded as higher than Chorus II in tessitura. In connection with performances of the work which have come to my attention, equality or inequality in the roles of the two Choruses seems not to have been an issue.

2. *Unity.* If a *text* has unity (for example, a fine poem) and each phrase of the text is set appropriately but without regard to a motivic

design or tonal plan, the result can produce a certain, if not complete, feeling of unity. Such a feeling can be greatly reinforced by employing some unified succession of keys, underlining the unity and what might be called the *rhetoric* of the text. (It is one of the miracles of Mozart that, in his operas, scene continuously follows scene with the utmost tonal freshness and meaningfulness, always buttressing the logic and unity of the long tonal plan.) In other words, the entire *Requiem* text could have been set without regard to a tonal center or to an ordered succession of keys. To underscore the unity and dramatic nature of the text, however, it seemed important to reinforce its rhetorical plan with a corresponding tonal rhetoric. For example, Part I, *Lamentations*, is in E minor (Phrygian) and is given over to an expression of mourning; since this mood never returns, no subsequent chorus is built on the tonality associated with it. Furthermore, since (for purposes of tonal unity) Part I, *Lamentations* virtually prescribes E major for the concluding movement, no movement preceding the final one anticipates the tonal center of that movement until the final cadence ("for ever and ever," p. 217) immediately preceding the fugal finale, in E major.

The problem in constructing a long work is not so much the planning of a logical succession of keys as it is the reconciliation of such a succession to the exigencies of music and text encountered along the way. A good key scheme may call for A major at a certain point: the text cries out for B-flat minor! In writing the *Requiem*, no preliminary tonal course was plotted. All that mattered was that the tonal center was to be E, because the climax of the final chorus, with the single and only high B, reached in the Sopranos (p. 240, meas. 120), was already in my mind and I worked backwards from that. On the other hand, in writing each successive chorus, I first looked back and then ahead, and asked myself, "Is this the right tonal block to build the structure and make it stand?" Here, in broad outline, is the tonal plan that resulted:

Part I   E minor
Part II   A minor through shifting tonalities to G
Part III   C, G, F, C
Part IV   A-flat, B-flat, D-flat, B-flat minor, D-flat, F, A-flat
Part V   C minor, C, A minor, A, E

The plan shows certain symmetries. The largest one frames the entire work: E minor and A minor for the first two movements and their tonal reflection, A major leading to E major, in the last two choruses of Part V.

No unifying motive or motto was used to bind the work together. Thematically, its unity is chiefly the unity of contrast. On the other hand, certain phrases do recur in varied versions: a) The passage for Chorus II, "Behold ye, regard, and wonder marvelously," occurs at the end of each of the last two movements of Part II, first in open then in close position. b) The passage for Chorus I, "The eternal God is thy refuge," reappears, extended and with different words, twice in Part II, "What man is he," once in Part IV, "I am their music," and once in Part V, further extended, at the words "He asked life of thee" (p. 216) —each reappearance being in a different key. c) The short antiphonal choral song with which Part IV begins also concludes it, in somewhat extended form. At the conclusion the words are different and the antiphony is confined to Chorus II alone, *divisi*, but the material and tonality are the same as at the beginning—all for the sake of unity.

Certain unifying thematic interrelations are also traceable. The phrase "How is it that ye have no faith?" from Chorus I (p. 46) is made rhythmic to form the principal theme of "Good tidings to the meek" (p. 70), and the bass line at this point becomes the subsidiary theme of the same movement. Also the subject for the fugue of Chorus II, "Blessed be the Lord God," (p. 112) is a variant of the subject for the fugue of Chorus I, "O let the nations be glad" (p. 83); though, in other respects, the two fugues are entirely different in both construction and feeling.

3. *Form.* In their beauty and flexibility, choral forms are a vast subject. Suffice it to say here that, in writing a succession of several choruses, variety of formal treatment is surely desirable. A long series of through-composed choruses would tend to lack shape: continuous use of any one kind of formal design—binary, ternary, rondo, or even fugue—would be monotonous. In writing the *Requiem*, no preconceived order of forms was laid down, but the value of formal contrast was kept in mind. As it turned out, the work contains little or no duplication of forms, as shown in the analytical section below. There is one shorter rondo form; one binary, one ternary form; one scherzo with trio; one round, etc. There are three fugues, but each of them has a different shape: "O let the nations be glad" (pp. 83 ff.) has *stretto* and augmentation (for dramatic reasons); "Blessed be the Lord God" (pp. 112 ff.) is (again for dramatic reasons) as compact as possible (28 measures) and is framed between a sonorous augmentation of the Answer and a sonorous augmentation of the Subject; and the concluding fugue (pp. 218 ff.) employing both Choruses, is built on a modulating subject beginning, exceptionally, on the third degree, with a subdominant answer. Chorus II carries this final fugue forward, and, in addition to the usual developmental episodes, Chorus I interpolates new material in the form of a more homophonic Alleluia against the Amen of Chorus II.

4. *Tempi.* The usual alternation of slow and fast movements is an

esthetically sound principle. But it is one thing to write an instrumental *Allegro-Adagio-Allegro*, and quite another to maintain tempo contrasts in a choral work of some twenty separate movements, particularly when there is a text and the words dictate the rate of speed—now fast, now slow, and not necessarily in alternation. The desirability of such tempo contrasts was considered from the start, in preparing the text. In general, the tempi change from movement to movement. Variations on the usual slow-fast-slow are found in Part II, "What man is he" (pp. 45, ff.), where tempo changes occur within a single movement; in Part III, where the speed increases in three successive stages as Chorus I invites, entreats, and finally implores Chorus II to put on the "garment of praise"; and in Part V where, conversely, the tempi of each of the first four of its five movements grow successively slower. Groups of fast movements are not uncommon in music; groups of slow movements are rather rare, even dangerous. But in Part V we have reached the solemn moment of leave-taking, and the progressive slowness of these four movements is meant to convey the increasing sense of resignation, consolation, peace; then, by contrast with what follows, to heighten the sense of release, fullfilment, even joy, of the concluding *Allegro moderato*, "Amen and amen, alleluia."

Notes on the Individual Movements

Part I: *Lamentations*
  "Lamentations" *Adagio*

Even Chorus II is here divided into two equal four-part choruses in order to produce continuous waves of sound. Their overlapping yields, without undue difficulty for the singers, certain passing dissonances, such as those shown in Example 2, which, if isolated, would be hard to produce. On the face of it, certainly, they look rather unchoral.

EXAMPLE 2

Meas. 2   Meas. 12   Meas. 18   Meas. 51

The notes that occur *on* the beats are dissonant in themselves. In preparing the first performance, Professor Lawton began by rehearsing only those notes, omitting the triplet figures, to fix the basic progressions in the minds of the singers: a time-saving rehearsal device.

The subdivision of Chorus II into eight parts not only produces waves of lament: it has the additional advantage of making the unfluctuating, four-part block chords to which Chorus I is confined seem, by comparison, strong and firm in voicing words of consolation and promise.

It is perhaps significant, as a point of style, that no accidentals appear in this movement until the thirty-first measure. Then they pour forth—till, within six measures, every note of the scale has been flatted, either enharmonically or not, to color the words "Refrain thy voice from weeping and thine eyes from tears." The lowering of a single tone in this manner was a favorite expressive resource of the Renaissance. Here we might speak of a seven-fold manifestation of that resource.

This movement—which is broadly ternary, bordering on sonata form—is based on two contrasting musical ideas, one for each Chorus, corresponding to the two contrasting ideas of the text. Part I is the exordium of the whole work and sets forth the conflict that the ensuing movements are to resolve.

Part II: *The Triumph of Faith*
"Why make ye this ado?" *Allegro*, short rondo

Chorus I resumes the Phrygian mode used in Part I to whisper its question; Chorus II repeatedly replies in the Aeolian. The solicitude of Chorus I draws forth only anger and despair from the mourners. The music of both Choruses employs imitative writing but of opposite kinds: Chorus I, *fugato*, ascending in *stretto*, disjunct and *staccato*; Chorus II, *canonetto*, descending by fifths, conjunct and *legato*. A somber cadence, with low minor-third in the Tenors, concludes the mourners' dark replies (cf. the opening chord of Monteverdi's wondrous setting of Petrarch's sonnet *Hor ch'el Ciel e la Terra*, in his *Madrigali, Libro ottavo*, Malipiero ed., p. 39).

"What man is he that liveth and shall not see death?" *Allegro conciso* and *Lento tranquillo*

Chorus II now takes the initiative and vehemently defies Chorus I in a mounting series of questions of doubt and assertions of despair. At each new one the tonality rises from A minor up through the octave to A major (p. 55, meas. 48). Meanwhile Chorus I answers every challenge with increasing serenity and joy. Finally, amid the whisperings of the awestruck mourners, the faithful offer a living demonstration of eternal life: "O Lord, Thou hast brought up my soul from the grave; Thou hast kept me alive." And the mourners can only murmur, "Behold ye, regard, and wonder marvellously."

The movement is through-composed and shows many changes of texture: declamatory style, chordal style, chanting, clashing antiphony, whisperings, and exclamations in one Chorus against held chords in the other. Twice harmonic inversion is employed (meas. 5–7 and 13–15; meas. 35–37 and 40–42).

"Good tidings to the meek" *Poco andante*

After the amorphous form of the preceding movement, a more definite shape seemed called for. A simple, three-part-song form sets forth Isaiah's words of ineffable beauty. As mentioned above, the theme is a rhythmical variant of "How is it that ye have no faith?" and the Bass line that accompanies it becomes the subsidiary theme (meas. 12 ff.). In contrast to the prevailing tenderness, an *appoggiatura* figure stresses the poignancy of certain sorrowful words that appear successively: *broken-hearted* (meas. 17–21, A minor); *mourn* (meas. 26–31, G minor); *mourning* (meas. 45–49, B minor). Once more, as the song ends, Chorus II murmurs "Behold ye, regard, and wonder marvellously."

Part III: *The Call to Song*
"Be filled with the spirit" *Lento e sereno*

This is the first of four successive movements of Part III in which the faithful, with increasing intensity, urge the mourners to sing, to praise God, to put on "the garment of praise for the spirit of heaviness."

In preparation for writing this first movement, the text was first set as a round for women's voices. The setting was not used note for note, but it is to be found in measures 18–26 (omitting measures 23 and 24, which were inserted to extend the cadence). The first line of the round is given out first; then the second is added to it (meas. 9–14), the cadence varied; and finally the third line is added to the first two and the cadence extended. Following each of these three entreaties the men's voices comment on the ensuing silence. Their voice-parts, like those of the round, also increase in number: first two, then three, then four. Chords of the Neapolitan sixth (meas. 8, 17, 29) offer a contrast to the diatonic round and color the short phrases. This simple movement took a disproportionate number of days to write (five), the problem of timing was so important.

"O let the nations be glad" *Andante piacevole*

The entreaties of Chorus I become more urgent in the course of this fugue, by means of *stretti*. In the middle section, the subject appears in canon at the octave below (meas. 19–22) and again at the fifth below (starting at meas. 27) as the *stretto* section proper begins. This canon is then presented in the subdominant and against it the Alto has a third canonic entrance with accents displaced—in Renaissance terminology, *per arsin et thesin*. While this continues, the Soprano enters (meas. 36) with the normal subject, to be answered by the Bass after one beat, in canon at the compound fourth below, again with accents displaced. This canon at the fourth below is repeated between Alto and Tenor (meas. 39) and to it is added, after one beat, a canon at the second above in the Soprano. This leads to another triple canon (meas. 43), also one beat apart (Bass, Soprano, Alto), but here the canon is at the compound fifth and octave above. Finally (meas. 46) a triple canon at the fifth below and seventh above is presented in augmentation, and against the three augmented forms (in dominant, tonic, and subdominant) the Alto enters with the tonic subject in its original note values. All told, the complete subject appears in canon with itself— *a* 2, *a* 3, *a* 4—in at least eight different ways, all purely accidental; for its canonic possibilities were totally unforeseen. The melody, the subject of the fugue, was conceived without any thought of its possible *stretti*, purely as an appropriate setting of the text. After the exposition was written, the possible *stretti* became apparent and were then utilized for their dramatic value. The canons did not shape the tune: the tune yielded the canons. Following the cadence of the fugue, the three lower voices darkly record the continued unresponsiveness of the mourners, and the call to song grows louder and more impassioned in the movement that follows.

"Sing unto Him" *Allegro con spirito*

The form of this movement is not easy to categorize. Four elements are presented in the first twenty-four measures: short imitative commands, roulades, a chordal chant, dactylic chords in close alternation. All of these elements are then transposed, rescored, extended, and intensified throughout twice the original number of measures, culminating in a *tutti* command, "Sing unto him", in which the downward leaps of the initial motive are expanded to an octave, in augmentation.

The faithful can scarcely plead further. In desperation they cry "Utter a song," then ask in anguish, "Can I hear any more the voice of singing men and singing women? Can I? Any more? Any—" and the mourners finally break forth into song: "Blessed be the Lord God, Who only doeth wondrous things." (This text was chosen, from among several other appropriate ones, for its explosive initial letter *B*.) Against a bell-like motive in the Sopranos and Tenors and over a dominant pedal in the Basses, the Altos of Chorus II give out, in the dominant, the subject of the ensuing fugue. The prolonged dominant preceding it reflects, rhetorically, the question, which is still being asked by Chorus I. The musical answer to that question comes when the tonic is sounded at the opening of the fugue itself (*Allegro giusto*, p. 112). To balance the initial dominant pedal, a tonic pedal leads to the final cadence (pp. 118–119). The dominant pedal accompanied the question: the tonic pedal underlines the answer. Chorus I re-enters to join in singing the same text as Chorus II. The bell-like motive rings back and forth between Sopranos I and II, and the Tenors of both Choruses unite to proclaim the augmented subject, now in the tonic. At *Largamente* (p. 119) the Tenors separate again to form a broad and sonorous eight-part Myxolydian cadence. The final C-major chord interlocks the men's and women's voices for maximum sonority.

Part IV: *The Garment of Praise*
"Sing with the spirit" *Lento e devoto*

A short antiphonal song, like a responsive prayer, opens this section with the words of St. Paul—the perfect motto for all singers: "I will sing with the spirit and I will sing with the understanding also." To differentiate the sound of the quiet injunctions of Chorus I from that of the quiet answers of Chorus II promising to observe them, Chorus I sings chiefly in close position, and Chorus II responds chiefly in open. As a result, though the material of each successive injunction is mirrored in different voices of the responses (e.g., p. 121), the effect is not one of a continual four-part chorus but of two such choruses conversing in contrasting sonorities.

"Let everything that hath breath" *Allegro*

In recitatives, the Baritones now call for one manifestation of praise after another. Choruses I and II respond together as an eight-part choir, in a series of movements which draw upon various resources of this incomparable choral medium.

In the first such movement (*Più mosso*, p. 127) at the words "Break forth into singing," Chorus I answers Chorus II with full imitation but not antiphonally. Horn-like figures metaphorically illustrate the words "mountains" and "forest."

The second such movement, "Let them give glory," is more extended. At the words "Let the earth rejoice," Chorus I answers Chorus II antiphonally. The form of this movement is that of a scherzo-trio-scherzo, with a short coda drawn from the trio. The texture of the trio contrasts in every way with that of the scherzo. All eight parts are involved. Some supply the harmonic background, while others sing in canon with each other. The tune yields four little "canons two-in-one" (A II and B I, S I and T II, S II and T I, S I and T II; in B-flat minor, G-flat, B-flat minor and F minor respectively); then four "canons four-in-one" (S II, T I, A I, B II; S I, T II, S II, A II; A I, B I, A II, T I; A II, B I, A I, B II; in A-flat, F minor, D-flat, G-flat and B-flat, respectively). In all, each of the eight parts has the tune three times, except A II (four times) and B II (twice). In interpreting this trio-section, it has proved helpful to think of the repeated quarter-note chords as resembling the strumming of a big guitar. The imitative entries and the repeated eighth-notes of the harmonic background are meant to convey an impression of the multitudinous isles.

"Praise Him all ye stars of light" *Recitative*

This is the third such hortatory movement. The Baritones now exhort all heaven and earth to praise. The Sopranos and Altos form a four-part women's chorus at the words "the morning stars sang together" (p. 151). The sustained high F's in Sopranos I illustrate the word "stars" and the humming in the three lower voices is to suggest the stars' singing together—distant, undulating music of the spheres. As it fades away, a corresponding four-part men's chorus breaks in *forte* at the words "and all the sons of God shouted for joy" (p. 153). This is answered literally by the women's chorus, after which the phrase "shouted for joy" is tossed back and forth in rapid alternation between the men's and the women's voices, instead of the more usual antiphonal disposition employing two identical mixed choruses.

This passage leads to the fourth and climactic chorus of praise (pp. 158 ff.). The text (*The Wisdom of Solomon*, 19:9), depicts the frenzied joy of the Israelites after crossing through the Red Sea: "For they went at large like horses, and leaped like lambs, praising Thee, O Lord." The form of the movement consists of two main sections of, surprisingly enough, equal length: the first thirty measures set forth three musical ideas corresponding to the three parts of the text; the last thirty measures repeat them in a different series of tonalities and different scoring, with the roles of the two Choruses interchanged. The texture is predominantly one of *cori spezzati*, but the antiphony is produced by several different numbers and combinations of voices of contrasting timbres. For example, at the opening (p. 158) S I and II, A II, T II, and B II are answered by A I and II, T I and II and B I; then the two Choruses answer each other in the normal manner (p. 160); then five upper voices are answered by four lower (pp. 161–162); later seven parts are answered by four (p. 168). At "praising Thee, O Lord" (p. 170) the four-part women's chorus is answered by the four-part men's chorus. Finally a five-part grouping is answered (for the first time) by all eight parts (p. 174), a texture that concludes the movement in a climactic setting of the words.

The faithful have indeed triumphed. In hushed tones they sing, "I am their music, and now am I their song." The setting of these words (pp. 176–178) is a variant of the three sustained passages in Part II: "The eternal God" (p. 48), "His anger endureth but a moment" (p. 61) and "O Lord, Thou hast brought up my soul" (p. 67). The long melismatic phrase is used there for the words "everlasting," "life," and "alive," respectively; here it is used for the word "song."

The music with which Part IV began now concludes it, with a slight interpolation that leads the voices a little higher (meas. 23 and 24; "with my whole heart"). The final chord is rearranged for eight notes—two different open-position chords, interlaced without doubling —to bring out the words assigned to each, both, by good fortune, ending with -*ing*. The delicacy of the whole reprise is meant to be enhanced by being sung by Chorus II alone, divided (as in Part I) into eight parts, but (in performance) all hands generally prefer to join in.

Part V: *The Leave-taking*

The concluding section has five movements, the first and last being for double chorus.

"Ye were sometimes darkness" *Lento e cupo*

Beginning in C minor, the introduction is given out by Chorus I. Darkness is suggested by use of the voices' lower registers and by the succession of no less than ten cross-relations in measures 3–7. The tone color changes completely with the antithesis "but now are ye light in the Lord"—a further instance of seeking to match musical and textural rhetoric. A deceptive cadence leads to a D-minor chord and Chorus I repeats the introduction, almost note for note, a tone higher. This would have led to E minor but for an extension which leads to C major, at which point the movement proper—a march—begins. It extends through 86 measures, with the sole words "Walk as children of light." The movement is organized on large dimensions. Essentially monothematic, though not a fugue, its tonal structure is, nevertheless, basically fugal (even more so than the structure of my *Alleluia*). Briefly, the structure is: tonic—dominant—episode; relative minor—episode; subdominant—dominant pedal and episode; tonic—codetta with tonic pedal. The eight voice-parts are entirely independent except at the climaxes of the three episodes where two descending inner lines reinforce each other for expressive purposes (meas. 48–51, 65–69, 88–95). In the second episode, the climax is built by seven successive imitative entrances (starting with Alto I, meas. 59–66). This device, so dear to the hearts of sixteenth-century composers, appears nowhere else in the *Requiem*. The result is anything but sixteenth century in sound. Another device, of which Lassus and his forebears were very fond, was the avoidance of parallel fifths between two successive triads by crossing voices. This device is used many times here (e.g., meas. 30) but again without any suggestion of sixteenth-century music, perhaps because of the immediate return to the first triad, and perhaps because the harmony at the second triad is always IV over V. This ancient scoring of the recurring triadic motive adds to its lightness, resilience, and ease of execution. The movement as a whole is pictorial. At the close, the little procession of children fades away in the distance.

"The Lord shall be unto thee" *Largo*

This and the preceding movement both refer to "light" and so here the opening phrase derives from the preceding movement. At the third measure, a tonic pedal-point (F above middle C) starts in Tenors, passes, with automatically less intensity, to the Altos, then—again automatically with still less—to the Sopranos, continuing throughout the movement, to illustrate the words "an everlasting light." At *Solenne* (meas. 10), reference to the tonic minor underscores the solemnity of the words.

"Return unto thy rest" *Poco adagio*

In a movement almost wholly consonant, the faithful now take their leave, propitiated, their errand of mercy performed. In place of dissonance, many pauses and frequent modulations through chords of the Neapolitan sixth (meas. 2 and 3; 7–11; 20–22) portray the longing for rest. At *Molto sostenuto* (meas. 26) root-position chords, with Tenor and Alto constantly crossing, ascend by whole-steps throughout the gamut—and beyond—to portray the leave-taking. Then, too, at the word "soul" two voices drop out in the resolution of the dominant (meas. 6); then three drop out (meas. 14); and, at the final cadence, four drop out and only Soprano I sounds the resolution, suggesting, progressively, the soul's disembodiment. This movement would never be mistaken for the work of the Divine Claudio, but I could never have written it if I had not studied with him—as I somehow like to feel I did.

"Thou has given him" *Lento e tranquillo*

Chorus II responds with serene resignation. This movement, finding the words of which ended my search for an elegiac text, is through-composed. The first sentence is set darkly for the three lower voices, with divided Basses. At the second sentence (meas. 10) the Sopranos enter and the setting here is the fifth version of the recurring passage first heard with the words "The eternal God is thy refuge" (Part II, p. 48). The melismatic passage, here used for the words "Thou gavest him a long life," is now longer than in any of the previous versions. At the words "even for ever and ever," three root-position chords descending by thirds (one of the calmest progressions in music) lead to a long plagal cadence (one of the gentlest of all closes).

"Amen and amen, alleluia" *Allegro moderato*

The *Requiem* has been called "a happy song of death." Certainly here all is joy. One hesitates to analyze it, but for a few pertinent facts.

Writing a fugue for double chorus is a fascinating problem. If a long subject is chosen and carried consistently through all eight parts, the fugue will run to great length, like those colossal ones of Sarti and Cherubini quoted in the latter's *Counterpoint and Fugue*. On the other hand, a short subject, running through all eight parts, produces reasonable length but tends to be rather epigrammatic, like those in Martini's *Saggio*, one of which, by Filippo Baroni, is only 39 measures long.[1] Bach, in the first section of his eight-part motet, *Singet dem Herrn*, solved the problem by employing a long subject and writing a fugue for only four of the eight voices, the other four embellishing it contrapuntally or reinforcing certain lines.

Another possible solution for a fugue for double chorus concludes the present work. To continue the personification of the two choruses, the final movement of the *Requiem* is really a four-voiced fugue for Chorus II in which the episodes are largely replaced by the interpolation of a more homophonic and wholly independent *Alleluia*, sung first by Chorus I, then by both Choruses together. How often a song, in whole or in part, has found its way into a larger composition! The music of this *Alleluia* was written, July 18–24, 1957, a few months before the *Requiem*, as part of a song called *The Passenger*. This song is a setting of a poem that was written by Mark Anthony de Wolfe Howe on his ninetieth birthday. In the song, there are two piano interludes that suggest a distant angelic choir. These interludes were later transcribed for four-part chorus and incorporated into the fugal finale of the *Requiem*, as episodes.

A few technical details of this fugal finale might be mentioned. The subject begins, rather exceptionally, on the third degree. Though the subject modulates to the dominant, it has a subdominant answer. In the relative-minor section, however, the answer is in the dominant (meas. 37) and would have run too far afield if the expected cadence had not been avoided (meas. 40 and 41).

In its final appearance, the *Alleluia* is rescored antiphonally for both Choruses (p. 237). At the climax (p. 240) they join forces in a free eight-part texture of maximum sonority, which is preserved—as the melody descends—by the gradual doubling and reinforcing of parts (p. 241). This is followed by the coda (*Lento e sereno*, p. 242). Here, the *Amen* of the fugue subject and the melody of the *Alleluia*, though they had been conceived independently, are combined by Alto I and Soprano II. The final cadence (meas. 134–136) is an extension of the final cadence of Part I (*Adagissimo*, p. 31) transformed by the singular beauty of the *u*-sound in a soft "Alleluia." In the two inter-

[1] The work is quoted in its entirety in Alfred Mann, *The Study of Fugue* (New York: Norton, 1965), pp. 305–312.

woven E-major chords at the end, the *Alleluia* of one chorus floats above the *Amen* of the other, the chorus of mortals.

L'envoi

In the opening paragraph of this essay, I mentioned that during the summer of 1954 I had been looking for an elegiac text. Let me explain why.

In June, 1954, Frederick S. Pratt II, a young choral conductor whom I did not know though our families were old friends, telephoned to ask if he might come to see me about getting some sort of conducting job. He had studied music at Harvard and at Yale and had recently returned from Copenhagen where, as a Fulbright Fellow, he had had an inspiring year of choral studies under the distinguished Dr. Mogens Wøldike. Fred wanted to share that experience with others. But he had just learned that he had only four to six months to live.

Next day he came to see me and we had a good talk. After the first few minutes, it was clear that he had the highest choral standards. "I've gotten so much out of music," he said enthusiastically, "I want to put something back into it." The more he talked, the more I hoped a job could be found for him. But it was June, when jobs are scarce, and I was just going away. I'd try, but could promise nothing. We agreed to exchange letters during the summer, and after an hour he left, calling back "Cheerio!" as he drove off.

By luck, I found two possible jobs for him, but they were too far away from where he had to be. During the summer I wrote him a couple of long letters about choral music and choral standards; but he was not up to answering them.

After returning home in the fall, I wrote again, to let him know that the things he had said in June had given me an idea for an extended choral work and that I was going to write it. This, I hoped, would give him the assurance that he had, in truth "put something back into music."

The letter reached his house the day after he died. The *Requiem* was written in fulfillment of the promise the letter contained.

Randall Thompson and the Music of the Past

by James Haar

Some years ago Randall Thompson mentioned to me in the course of a conversation that he was working on a new choral piece. "In what style?" I asked. "In my same old style" was the reply. The question was clumsily put; I had meant to ask about the kind of chorus to be used, or whether the fabric was to be more contrapuntal than chordal, or what the dimensions of the work were to be. The answer, from this man too kind to exercise his wit at a friend's expense, was honest and only in part self-deprecating. For Randall Thompson's large and varied list of compositions, the product of more than fifty years of creative work, has a sure-footed unity of style and rhetoric that transcends differences between individual pieces and that stands as a monument of calm integrity in a musically turbulent half-century.

Of course, this music has its roots in the past. It is, in fact, strongly academic in nature; but here the reader must note that I mean the term in a sense completely free of the pejorative connotations it ordinarily carries. When Thompson's Third Symphony received its first performances in Boston in 1949, Allen Sapp urged the Harvard undergraduates who were members of Thompson's and Sapp's counterpoint classes to go hear it, telling them that they would hear a work not only beautiful in its own right but also the kind of piece that a man who was in love with the study and teaching of counterpoint would write. I was then a student in Randall Thompson's course in modal counterpoint; I went to hear the symphony and found that Allen Sapp was right and that he had put the case very well. What he said about the symphony is even more applicable to the choral music: Randall Thompson's choral works are a shining reflection of the joy and creative skill with which he taught musical craft—of Palestrina and Lasso, of Monteverdi and Schütz, of Bach and Handel. It has been his belief that much of this craft is timeless in its nature, can form part of the basis of a composer's working vocabulary without loss to his individual talent. In this he is a true classicist and an academic in the best sense.

How should a musicologist view an unabashed twentieth-century exponent of the *stile antico*? I think that an impartial assessment, un-colored by nineteenth-century views about progressive art, is in order. The still young discipline of musicology, like many a precocious child, has developed great expertise in some areas while remaining somewhat adolescent in others. Thus enormous—if still insufficient—effort has been spent on stylistic analysis that shows, for example, how Palestrina's music differs from the *stile antico* of the seventeenth and eighteenth centuries (no equivalent effort has been made to demonstrate how Jos-quin or Willaert differ from Palestrina). This is important and valid work; but it need not be accompanied, as it often has been, by denigra-tion of the "strict style" and its highly skilled practitioners. The *seconda prattica* of Monteverdi is more dramatic and more glamorous than the music of Palestrina's Roman pupils; but Monteverdi's own music is evidence that the *prima prattica* was still a vehicle for imaginatively creative work, as is shown in his Mass based on Gombert's motet *In illo tempore*. Seventeenth-century composers turned to the contrapuntal style of the preceding century for a variety of reasons, but they certainly meant for the music they wrote in this style to stand on its own merits, as indeed the best of it does; two years ago, in the great Romanesque cathedral of Lund in southern Sweden, I heard a performance of Buxtehude's *Missa brevis* that sounded splendid, the work's slight anachronisms when compared with Palestrina hurting it not at all.

Bach's devotion to the music of the past is well known. His rela-tionship to the *stile antico*, the subject of thorough and loving attention in a recent study by Christoph Wolff,[1] is nowhere more magnificently displayed than in the cantus firmus treatment and the spacious fugal writing of the *Mass in B Minor*. For Bach, the strict style meant not only the contrapuntal rules of the sixteenth century, but also the music of his seventeenth-century predecessors; it was thus deliberately ec-lectic in nature. By a natural extension of this process, composers from Mozart through Mendelssohn and Schumann to Brahms chose late Baroque music, especially that of Bach and Handel, as their *stile antico* (the Palestrina revival of the nineteenth century, important for his-torical reasons, has not yet been much studied in regard to the quality of music that it produced).

Another aspect of nineteenth-century classicism was the retention and reuse of eighteenth-century formal patterns, sometimes in con-junction with features of Baroque style. Thus, in *Elijah* Mendelssohn wrote a chorus, "He watching over Israel," that is close to sonata form. Other examples such as the fourth movement of Schumann's *Rhenish* Symphony, neo-Baroque in polyphony but not in harmonic or formal design, or the closing chorus of the Brahms *Requiem*, again in a kind

[1] *Der stile antico in der Musik Johann Sebastian Bachs*. Studien zu Bachs Spätwerk (Wies-baden, 1968).

of sonata form, could be cited. Among the works of twentieth-century neo-classicists there are, of course, a great many instances of what would seem to be the same sort of thing; actually it is not, because in nearly all the neo-classical composers the emphasis, whether serious or satirical, is on the newness of the wine being poured into old bottles.

Composers living and working in academic surroundings—now a nearly universal pattern—were fairly numerous even in the earlier part of the twentieth century. The fact that echoes of Brahms, next of Fauré, then of Hindemith were often heard in the works of such men gave rise to the notion that academicians were conservatives pure and simple. For the past thirty years or so that has been a rather dated view, and recently some of us have come to feel the reverse—to categorize academic composers as men wilfully, sometimes perhaps perversely, inclined toward cerebral experiment, so much so that the "nach Bach" compositions of a few present-day composers are viewed with almost the same trepidation that the most totally serialized music calls forth. To turn back to the past after having resolutely shunned it is not easy; so different is one's perspective that the past itself seems to have changed.

For Randall Thompson it would seem that a good deal of the *Angst* of the modern composer-academic has not been an issue. When forming his own style, he was keenly aware of what other composers, particularly Americans of his own generation, were doing;[2] and his consciousness of our own musical past—dealt with by Elliot Forbes elsewhere in this volume—has become an important and lasting element in the development of his musical personality. This I think is evident in all his choral works, not just those on American themes, and can be seen in the cut of themes, in aspects of phrase structure, and in details of harmonic treatment. But if some of the musical rhetoric is American, a good deal of it is international and rooted in more than one temporal period, and this seems to me the result of his study and teaching of a wide spectrum of music.

When teaching modal counterpoint, Thompson is steeped in Palestrina and Lasso; in tonal counterpoint he shows his deep knowledge of Bach and especially of Handel. His courses in choral composition include all this and a good deal more, the elements of good part-writing and effective massing of sound drawn from the rich choral repertory that he knows so well and has contributed to so steadily. If nineteenth-century music has received less frequent mention from him, this is understandable; like most composers of his generation, Randall Thompson has felt the need to break loose from the hold of the nineteenth century. In this regard he has taken an individual position; in contrast with, say, Schoenberg, who retained much of the expressive rhetoric

[2] See, for example, his "The Contemporary Scene in American Music," *The Musical Quarterly*, XVIII (1932), pp. 9–17.

of the nineteenth century while searching for a new vocabulary of sound, Thompson has advocated, and practiced, use of conventional sounds in a fresh context, freed as much as possible of their nineteenth-century connotations.

As a graduate student in the mid-1950's, I studied choral composition with Randall Thompson at a time when he was writing a large choral piece. I remember the course with affectionate gratitude for what I learned from him; and I think of the *Mass of the Holy Spirit*, written at this time, as a fine example of the sound advice about choral techniques he gave us put into practice. The work also illustrates in general and in detail many aspects of Thompson's relationship to older music.

An English Mass or Communion Service, the *Mass of the Holy Spirit* is written for four voices *a cappella*. There is relatively little use of divided choirs, and in general the work is less virtuosic in style than, say, the *Requiem* or the large works on Gospel texts. Its dimensions are those of a sixteenth-century Mass, and most of the movements are congruent in general stylistic matters and in disposition of voices with sixteenth-century polyphony—to my mind more that of Lasso than of Palestrina. Many melodic and harmonic figures are in fact the same, or nearly so, as those used in the sixteenth century. Of course, the work does not sound like a Mass by Lasso; this is in no sense textbook music. Presently I shall try to isolate a few of the ways in which the composer bends the material into an aural shape all his own.

In ways that, as I have tried to show above, have honored precedents, the work contains elements drawn from periods other than the sixteenth century. Thus the *Gloria* is cast in a resplendent neo-Baroque mold, the sopranos singing *"quasi trombe"* their hymnic fanfares over a churning pentatonic *moto perpetuo* in the lower voices. And the "Hosanna" is a rollicking Handelian *fugato*, with its triple meter the only reminder of sixteenth-century practice. The musical "peaceable kingdom" in which these apparently disparate elements dwell together in full aesthetic harmony is in itself proof of the composer's belief that diverse elements of the past can be combined to give new results.

The formal patterns of the five movements are in large part dictated by the text and thus correspond, as in the *Sanctus*, with both Renaissance and Baroque practice. But the ternary scheme of the *Gloria*, the elements of variation-chain in the *Credo*, and the close-to-sonata structure of the *Kyrie* are deliberate choices, deliberately not following the through-composed method of the sixteenth century. Thompson's careful preoccupation with form is well known; he talks about this, more convincingly than I can, in his essay on the *Requiem* (the second paper in this volume).

Nor are the phrase structures for the most part those of Renaissance music, though they approach it more closely than they do the sequential spinning-out of Baroque polyphony. Here some of the native Anglo-American element in the composer's style doubtless shows through, for passages in ingenious double counterpoint such as bars 16 ff. of the *Kyrie* turn out to be four-bar phases, and many of the supple and subtle approaches to cadential points are heard as extensions of a symmetrical, tune-dominated phrase structure. This is surely a conscious choice, and is thus another of the ways in which Thompson creates a blend of stylistic elements peculiarly his own.

A few details in the Mass may be singled out as illustrations of how the composer has adapted and breathed new life into aspects of the *stile antico*. Like many fluent musicians past and present, Randall Thompson is fond of species counterpoint and aware of its great usefulness to students. In the "Benedictus" of the *Mass* he shows some of the uses to which skill in this art may be put (see Ex. 1). This section begins with something close to strict fourth species, its Mixolydian melodic cast adding to its "correctness." At bar 226 the suspensions and, now, *appoggiaturas* start to compound each other; the technique has hardly

EXAMPLE 1

changed, but the sound, one of superimposed harmonies, is pure Thompson. A melodic sequence, in second species, leads upward, adding as it goes the flowing quarter-notes of third species; the characteristic leisurely descent from the climax is again chiefly second species, leading to a cadence on the major second degree, a modern adaptation of sixteenth-century "chromatic" style.

EXAMPLE 2a

Use of chromaticism through unexpected juxtapositions of root-position chords was common in the second half of the sixteenth century, and was certainly not practiced solely by "modernists" such as Gesualdo and Monteverdi; even Palestrina used it, and so did Lasso. Randall Thompson's version of this technique, at once more modern and more tonally oriented, may be seen if one compares Example 2a, from Lasso's *Prophetiae Sibyllarum*, with the opening of the *Credo* in Thompson's *Mass* (Ex. 2b).

EXAMPLE 2b

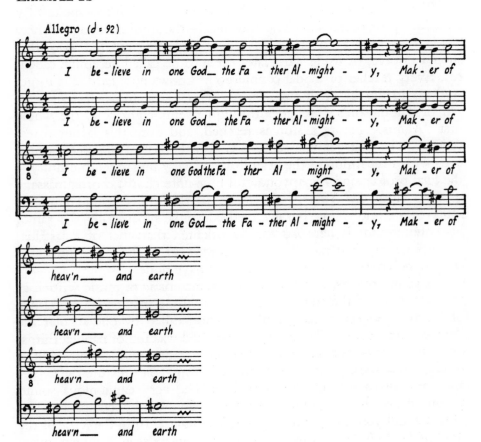

Canonic writing, beloved of Renaissance and Baroque composers alike and a favorite device of the *stile antico*, is beguilingly used in the

"Christe" of the *Mass*, a three-voice canon at the fourth below. While solving with his customary adroitness the tonal problems caused by the fourth-plus-fourth-equals-seventh, Thompson wrote a section of deliberately bland innocence, a perfect "Christe" foil to the troubled sound of the opening and closing "Kyries." Incidentally, when canons of this kind occur in sixteenth-century music, thorny problems of *musica ficta* arise, causing puzzlement and giving rise to elaborate arguments over where to add flats. To see Randall Thompson cutting these Gordian knots by simply placing flats where he evidently thought they sounded best may discomfit the learned tribe: what if that is what Josquin and Willaert and company did?

The great sixteenth-century theorist Gioseffo Zarlino spoke of a technique composers of his time often used—the art of avoiding cadences (*fuggir le cadenze*) by overlapping voices, dropping out the voice that should resolve, or using what later came to be called deceptive cadences. Every teacher of modal counterpoint knows how hard it is to get students to do this with any success. As a lesson to us all, the *Agnus Dei* of Thompson's *Mass* goes through twenty-eight bars, the whole first "Agnus," before a stop is reached, and even this is not a real cadence. The first genuine cadence is also the last of the piece, which ends with a repetition of the beautiful (and very un-sixteenth-century— the final progression has a wonderful blue-note chord) chordal passage used to close the *Kyrie* of the *Mass*. In this movement Thompson achieves Zarlino's aim, but by methods only superficially the same; his counterpoint is here *less* tonally oriented than that of Palestrina, all lines taking their melodic course somewhat in the way a fifteenth-century polyphonist like Ockeghem may have done.

A sound that was both new and characteristic of music written at the beginning of the sixteenth century was one marked by avoidance of fourths between voices, a phenomenon called by one scholar the "non-quartal" style.[3] The music that resulted was full of parallel thirds, or better, tenths, between outer voices, with one middle voice taking thirds, fifths, sixths, but never fourths. In four-voice texture the avoidance of fourths was nearly impossible. The very euphonious sound produced by this technique was much favored by composers like Obrecht and Josquin. If one looks at Example 3, from the *Kyrie* of the *Mass of the Holy Spirit*, this old technique can be seen in a new guise: parallel tenths between outer voices, parallel thirds between alto and tenor (if the alto is omitted real non-quartal three-voice texture results). The fact that in Example 3 the harmony consists of a chain of seventh chords seems as much—perhaps more—the result of the paired thirds and tenths as it does use of a particular chordal palette.

[3] C. W. Fox, "Non-Quartal Harmony in the Renaissance," *The Musical Quarterly*, XXXI (1945), pp. 33–53.

EXAMPLE 3

This seems important to me, for Randall Thompson's music is full of seventh-chord chains. They give a twentieth-century sound, true, plus a certain bittersweet flavor; but they also enormously facilitate the writing of full yet independently active four-voice texture. And it is in the sense of a sonorously effective musical technique, without pre-existent expressive overtones, that they are best understood, just as are equivalent techniques in earlier music.

I hope that these examples will suffice to show something of what I mean by Randall Thompson's relationship to the great choral music of the past. The job of the historian is in large part one of separating and assigning labels to individual elements in a work of art. We can, indeed ought to, attempt some kind of synthesis on the basis of evidence provided by our analytical efforts; but it would be mistaken as well as presumptuous to assume that our process of disassembly and reassembly in any way duplicates the way the artist worked—let alone what he had in mind at the beginning, the end, or at any point in the compositional process. Only the music itself can give us adequate response to our queries; but the next best thing is to hear from the composer himself, as we have in the preceding essays. I will close with one generalization: it is dangerous in a work of art to get so close to the past that labels can be stuck on, for one's meaning may be mistaken, one's seriousness or candor impugned; because of this I should like to pay special tribute to Randall Thompson's sophisticated skill but still more to the integrity, openness, and good manners of his musical personality, which together have placed his music in a safe harbor beyond these dangers.

Psalm and Gospel Settings

EDITORIALS

On three occasions, editorials in the *American Choral Review* were devoted to choral works by Randall Thompson. The works concerned represent a single decade—the 1960's—and they are also bound together by the choice of scriptural texts.

The composer wrote several Psalm settings during this period. The complete text of Psalm 23, *The Lord is my Shepherd*, was composed for four-part chorus with keyboard or harp accompaniment, and published for women's voices (the original version) and for mixed chorus. The opening of Psalm 122, combined with verses from Habakkuk and Genesis, was issued as a four-part *a cappella* work, *The Gate of Heaven*, and is available in versions for women's voices, men's voices, and mixed chorus.

A Psalm of Thanksgiving is singled out for discussion here because, like the settings of texts from the Gospel according to Saint Luke, it is a work of larger proportions, and it shares with these pieces the scoring for chorus and orchestra.

All three works were written on commission, and since the dedications to a church, a school, and a chorus—each of them in its own way representing strong New England traditions—contribute towards a suggestion of the environment of the composer's work, the occasional character of the reviews has been maintained and their text has not been subjected to any essential change.

A.M.

The Nativity According to Saint Luke

Forasmuch as many have taken in hand to set forth in order a declaration of those things which are most surely believed among us, . . . it seemed good to me also, having had perfect understanding of all things from the very first, to write unto thee . . .

Luke I:1–3

With these words the evangelist dedicated his account of the gospel to a friend who shared his belief. Our thoughts returned to this inscription in attending the first performance of *The Nativity according to Saint Luke*, for a striking parallel indeed is the dedication of this new work to Christ Church, Cambridge, by a member of its congregation, Randall Thompson. To write new music for the nativity text of Saint Luke is a bold plan. These are verses that "many have taken in hand," but Randall Thompson's work shows the quality of perfect understanding of which the evangelist speaks: it measures up to the eternally vivid and touching presentation of the text on which it is based.

The work was composed for the 200th anniversary of the famous first colonial church in Cambridge, a landmark in New England's cultural and political history. When plans for the commemoration were made, the composer decided to set aside a year of his creative work to honor the occasion. The sacred drama he wrote was given its first performance under his direction at Christ Church on December 13, 1961.

It is a moving experience to see the interior of a church serve as a setting for the dramatized Nativity story—one realizes that church music has been without liturgical drama too long. The scenic require-ments are of great simplicity, but the economic use of color and motion that staging imposes upon the performance of this sacred music results in an impression that is at once delightfully bright and deeply reverent.

The choir (ten women, eight men, and thirteen boys in the per-formance at Christ Church) remains seated in the regular choir stalls, but the soloists present the dramatic action in their midst. The special performers needed can be mustered without much difficulty by the average church music organization: a solo quintet (Mary, Elizabeth, Zacharias, Simeon, the Angel Gabriel) and several minor roles. The orchestra (seated to one side) also reflects the composer's awareness of the limitations and challenges of present day church performance: string quintet (not string orchestra), woodwind quartet, two brass instruments, and kettledrums. The organ joins choir and orchestra only at the very end where, through an impressive integration of texts, the Gospel of Saint Luke turns to the lesser doxology and the dramatic action involves the congregation.

The musical language is original but it is not experimental: the composer has the courage to speak directly. Randall Thompson's best known earlier works were born out of the great twentieth-century revival of choral music, of which he became the strongest American exponent. The present work shows this background for his creative career. It combines the lyricism of *The Peaceable Kingdom* (1936), the grandeur of *The Testament of Freedom* (1943), and the impeccable poly-phony of the *Mass of the Holy Spirit* (1956). In the last major choral work preceding *The Nativity according to Saint Luke*—the *Requiem* for double chorus (1958)—the composer explored fully a principle tested in earlier choral works. He compiled his text from different portions of the Scriptures (as did Handel in evolving the style of his choral anthems), arranging them in such a manner that there is a forceful continuity formed by dramatic contrast; in fact, the entire *Requiem* is cast in the form of a dialogue between the two choirs. The composition of *The Nativity according to Saint Luke* is marked by two further decisive steps. It is the composer's first major scenic work—after the miniature opera *Solomon and Balkis* (1942)—and it is the first work for which he chose the text from the New Testament (as did Handel in *Messiah*).

Included in the text are the two outstanding poems from the Gospels: the Magnificat (Song of Mary) and the Nunc Dimittis (Song of Simeon). Both, true to the dramatic clarity of the work, serve for intensified characterization of solo roles. But the Nunc Dimittis culminates in an extended choral response in preparation for a Recessional, and the chorus, singing in unison recitation, in full *a cappella* harmony, in simple chordal style, and in brief sonorous fugati, forms the frame for the entire work.

This frame surrounds solo passages of infinite charm. Mary's and Elizabeth's roles are carefully delineated; Mary's high voice contrasted by a cello solo (the Annunciation Scene) and Elizabeth's mezzo contrasted by a flute solo (the Visitation Scene). The Pastoral Scene, drawn with beautiful freshness, ranks with its most famous counterparts; and the interpolated Lullaby, based on a poem from the time of King James, is a rare gem.

The composer mentioned after the performance that he had begun the composition of the work with the last scene in order to have a path clearly laid out. The listener senses this deliberate planning. The seven scenes of the work are spanned by the appearances of the Angel, who announces life and death and the victory of life over death. The action and the scenic contrasts are presented in judicious pacing, letting each role emerge clearly and in balance with the others—even the roles of Joseph and Anna the Prophetess, which are barely sketched, express great dramatic strength. But the most remarkable aspect of the work is its dramatic continuity. We know Saint Luke's account of the Nativity only in isolated scenes, single lines often forming the basis of magnificent works, but we have forgotten the unity and the logic of action contained in this text, which Randall Thompson's setting of *The Nativity according to Saint Luke* recaptures: the work is perfection of form.

The Passion According to Saint Luke

Alfred Einstein spoke of a growing cleavage between artist and public as a legacy of music in the Romantic Era, and we may think at times that this separation is bound to lead to a conflict beyond reconciliation. How wrong this conclusion is was suddenly brought to mind at the performance of a new American choral work at which the entire audience rose to thank the composer. For the one hundred and fiftieth anniversary of Boston's Handel and Haydn Society, which was founded in 1815, Randall Thompson was asked to write a work of concert length for chorus and orchestra to be given its first performance in Symphony Hall on the anniversary date.

The premiere of a work by Randall Thompson is an important event in American musical life under any circumstances. The appearance of *The Passion according to Saint Luke* is of special interest both from the point of view of the evolution of the composer's work and of the history of American choral music. The work forms a sequel to Randall Thompson's sacred drama *The Nativity according to Saint Luke*, composed in 1961, and shows the composer at the highest level of fusing choral and dramatic means.

The chorus is one of the original elements of drama. Its functions were all important in Greek tragedy: it provided framework, continuity, and interpretation. This importance was lost in the resurgence of drama through Baroque opera, for the very essence of the *dramma per musica* was soloistic expression. In spite of a conscious dramatic use of choral writing in the works of Monteverdi, Carissimi, Lully, and Purcell, we do not find true prominence of the chorus in drama re-established until we come to the choral art of Handel. But here the struggle of balancing the forces of drama shaped the heroic course of an unparalleled artistic career.

Baroque opera also determined the dramatic presentation of the Passion story. Yet here the chorus and choral performance assumed a different role. Based on traditions of the medieval play, the musical setting of the Passion text had become an entirely choral form in the *Motettenpassion* of the Renaissance: the roles of all protagonists were written in polyphonic style. And when solo roles emerged in the seventeenth century Passion Oratorio, the share of the chorus remained significant.

It is against this background that Randall Thompson's new work should be considered. Like the early choral Passion settings, its text contains no interpolated poetry; and since the terse narrative of Saint Luke offers extended solo parts only for men's voices, the traditional assignment of the Evangelist's role to a tenor part would have deprived the score of contrast and balance. Thus, the composer decided to use the chorus to represent both the crowd and the narrator. While this choice was prompted by formal considerations, the dramatic strength inherent in this situation of choral narration became the most inspiring force in the progress of the work, and such choral passages as "he found them sleeping for sorrow," "blasphemously spake they against him," and "it was about the sixth hour" are unforgettable.

The novel presentation of the Passion, in which chorus and symphony orchestra surround tenor and bass soli, leads the listener to a fresh understanding of the structure of the text. This is especially so because the plan of the work differs in one other important aspect from that known to us in the Passion Oratorio. It opens with the triumphal entry into Jerusalem. "This (like many other tragedies) runs counter to the ancient unities of time, place and action," wrote the composer in a prefatory note for the program, "but it provides a picture of Jesus, the young Rabbi, at the apex of his career, hailed by the jubilant throng and explains the reasons for the jealousy, rivalry and fear of him, which slowly but inexorably led to his death."

The choral drama that results is powerful and moving. The role of Jesus rises with remarkable immediacy against the joyous outcry "Blessed be the King that cometh in the name of the Lord," and it is carried with ever deepening characterization to the lament of the daughters of Jerusalem and the Last Words. The merging of scenes through which the end of the work is intensified and the overlapping of choral and soloistic passages stand in contrast to moments of exquisite lyricism which impress upon the listener an orchestral writing as undeniably Randall Thompson's own as his choral style. There is a subtle use of leitmotif technique and of manifold contrapuntal means. But the strongest quality of the work is its directness: the impressive clarity of its recitation, its pedal points, its *a cappella* phrases. It is straightforward and noble—a fresco drawn by the hand of a great artist.

A Psalm of Thanksgiving

Randall Thompson's *A Psalm of Thanksgiving* received its first performance under the direction of the composer on November 15, 1967, at the Centennial Concert of the New England Conservatory.

The oldest music school in the nation, the Conservatory was completing a century of history distinguished by names ranging from Busoni to Hovhaness. The centennial celebration, marked by the inauguration of Gunther Schuller as the Conservatory's new president, was the occasion of a three day Symposium—"The Conservatory Redefined"—for which an illustrious group of delegates was convened. The concept of the Conservatory in a changing world was the central subject of addresses and discussions. The event culminated, as it should, in music. And it was choral music which in a changing world held a place of unchanging importance.

Randall Thompson's work touches upon a lofty heritage of English church music: the psalm setting as concerted anthem. The choice of the text was prompted by the terms of the commission. Written for the chorus of the Conservatory, the score was to combine a mixed chorus with a chorus of children's voices. In deciding upon Psalm 107 combined from the Psalter and the King James Version, the composer found a text that suggested both medium and form, for the poetic structure is rendered by the recurring verse "Oh that men would praise the Lord for his goodness, and for his wonderful works to the children of men!" But what a wealth of choral text is unlocked in the verses surrounded by this ritornel! "He led them forth—He brought them out of darkness and the shadow of death, and brake their bands in sunder—He turneth the wilderness into a standing water—tell out His work with gladness." Each line and each word recalls classical choral language, and, in a word, the composer measures up to it. An orbit of euphony opens with the first chorus: "And gathered them out of the lands, from the east, and from the west, from the north, and from the south."

His writing is spacious and transparent, his diction is compelling, and his sense of form unerring. A series of choral movements (no solo numbers are included in the work) is surrounded by an opening and closing hymn setting, and it is in the change of the diverse choral forces that the most impressive moments of the work occur (Ex. 1).

EXAMPLE 1

Yet with sure strokes these forces are gathered into one, as they are against the orchestral portrayal of the "great waters" in the tutti declamation of the famous 23rd verse (Ex. 2).

EXAMPLE 2

Randall Thompson's writing has assumed a singularly firm place in the American musical scene and his works have given fresh meaning to the finest in choral tradition.

Americana

by ELLIOT FORBES

The group was singing the line "And that has made all the difference."
Differ-ence they were singing, and Thompson suggested they make it *differ-unce*. "It's an *uh* sound, an *o umlaut* sound," he said. "*Differ-unce* is the way English is spoken and the audience has to understand every word or some of them will undoubtedly fall asleep."

So wrote Otile McManus in the *Boston Globe* (April 30, 1974) of a rehearsal Randall Thompson was conducting with the Lincoln-Sudbury Regional High School Chorus of ninety in preparation for a concert on April 28, which included his *Alleluia, The Peaceable Kingdom*, and *Frostiana*.

The wit, the continuing care for detail, and the love of working with young people shine forth in this account. The next Sunday at Christ Church I had the first of two opportunities to see Randall Thompson in action myself. And I was moved by what I heard. It was a festival evening with his choral and organ works. After the offering he led the youth choir in "Velvet Shoes" and "Lullaby" from *The Nativity according to Saint Luke*, and "My Master Hath a Garden." After the central hymn, the mixed choir sang a group which opened with *The Last Words of David* and ended with *Alleluia*. At that time no one could have known that the very next Thursday many of us would be reassembled there for a memorial service for "Woody's" widow, Evelyn Woodworth. Characteristically, Randall offered to conduct some members of the Harvard University Choir in a musical tribute, *Alleluia*, the work that Woody (G. Wallace Woodworth) had introduced thirty-four years ago at Tanglewood. The composer's sense of dedication and concern for shaped choral beauty was expressed anew, and all those privileged to be present were uplifted.

The purpose of this paper is to salute the relationship between Randall Thompson and America. We will end up where we began: the composer-teacher serving the needs of young American choruses—*young* in spirit, at any rate—every time the association is made with his music, and, better still, with him at the helm interpreting his music. In between we will consider some lesser-known aspects of Thompson's life as a background to two more specific relationships with the American scene: one, the music he has written about America, its history or its mores, and two, his settings of American verse and a setting inspired by American art.

When he entered Harvard in the fall of 1916, Thompson tried out for the Harvard Glee Club and was rejected by its conductor, "Doc" (Archibald T.) Davison; his conclusion: "My life has been an attempt to strike back!" Doc taught him counterpoint, the history of choral music (in which course he *was* allowed to participate in afternoon sings that ranged from plainchant and Dufay to Debussy chansons); and his teacher took time outside of class to criticize his early efforts in choral music. But the greatest impact that Davison had on him was the man's taste, his cultivation of the choral legato, and his adoration of the great choral literature.

Upon graduation Thompson studied with Ernest Bloch for a short time before completing work for his Master's degree at Harvard. This teacher provided two influences, one short-term, one long. The richness of Bloch's style and the loud, long, and passionate flavor of his music stimulated the writing of experimental works like the Piano Sonata and the Suite for Piano. This period of searching was soon over. At the same time Bloch made upon his student a vital imprint of professionalism about composition and the act of composing, which he has retained to this day.

In Rome, where for three years he was a Fellow at the American Academy, Thompson heard many great choral performances which included madrigal sequences by Vecchi and others. "Why not compose a sequence of sacred pieces," he thought; and soon he put the idea into practice with *The Peaceable Kingdom*. At the same time was born, perhaps unconsciously, the idea of secular cycles of texts in English, which resulted in a number of works which we will also be considering. An immediate manifestation of this principle was the great sequence of settings of the *Odes* of Horace.

When he returned to this country to take up residence in Greenwich Village, his immediate concern was to take orders for music so that he could eat. From writing songs to order he was able to earn $1,600 in 1925–26 and over $2,000 in 1926–27, on the strength of which he got married. By fulfilling an order from the Neighborhood Playhouse for incidental music to *The Grand Street Follies*, he was able to include choral ensembles and thus again take up the development of his facility for choral writing.

During this period Thompson met Stephen Vincent Benét and was stimulated to read his *Tiger Joy*. When he received a commission to write something for the Women's University Glee Club of New York, Thompson found that there were four poems about Rosemary scattered through this collection. Here was the chance to create a cycle of American verse by a single author revolving around a single subject.

"Chemical Analysis" (the first chorus of *Rosemary*) shows how a wordless accompaniment can introduce, conclude and support successive lines of text, each introduced by a new voice—Alto I, Alto II, Soprano II, Soprano I. "A Sad Song" shows the art of a choral motto *a 2* alternating with imitative verse-setting *a 3*, ending with the motto's answer to the tonic by a fourth voice, Alto II, with the final line. The first line of "A Nonsense Song" ("Rosemary, Rosemary, let down your hair") is a rhapsodic rise and fall which, by its reappearance as a harmonic solution at the end, provides a framework for the intervening verses in driving six-eight rhythm. These middle two choruses with their light three-part texture reflect the spirit of the *balletto* or *canzonetta* of the Italian Renaissance.

The final chorus, "To Rosemary," shows how Thompson responds to a more involved, sectional text. The poem begins:

Not where the sober sisters
Walk like old twilights by the jasper sea,
Nor where the plump hunt of cherubs hollyhilloes
Chasing their ruddy fox, the sun, you'll be!

followed by four more lines listing what Rosemary is not. Then the release:

They'll give you a curl'd tuba, tall as Rumor
They'll sit you on a puff of autumn cloud,
Gilded-fantastic as your scorn and humor,
And let you blow that tuba much too loud.

Four concluding lines begin:

Three impudent seraph notes, three starry coals

The musical solution is Handelian in concept. The first section is slow and quiet, static with repeated sonorities. The negation expressed in the first eight lines of verse is reinforced by the "unreality" of no harmonic movement—the music floats on reiterated B minor sonorities (Ex. 1).

Then comes the release, brisk, forte and fugal, in which the preceding repeated note idea is transformed into the first six notes of a lively fugue subject (Ex. 2).

Its inversion introduces the second pair of lines, presented again in contrapuntal texture. The last two words of this section, "too loud," provide the dynamic marking, *fortissimo*, for the concluding section, which alternates majestic chordal progressions with contrapuntal fragments; one of these is an irreverent bugle-call figure, derived textually from the tuba ("tu-tu-tu-tu"), which provides just the touch of whimsy to realize in music the poet's intent.

EXAMPLE 1

In *Rosemary* a fusion has been established of Renaissance song, Handelian choral drama, and Thompson's own melodic and harmonic gifts, along with his own rhythmic response to textual accents. This fusion provides an ideal means for the setting of words, verse or prose; it constitutes the heart of Thompson's style, and the wonder is that he can make it work as well for slow movements as for fast, and as effectively for portraying humor, action, patriotism, or devotion.

EXAMPLE 2

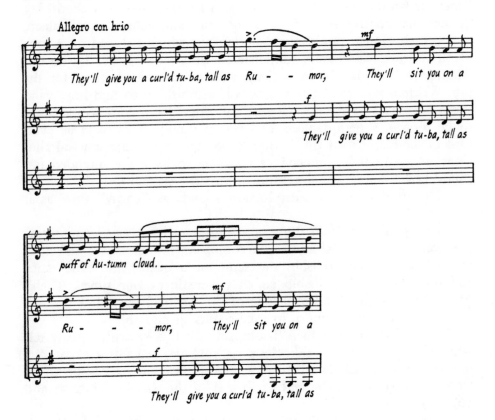

Humor reaches its high point in a sequence of five choruses whose texts have been gleaned from H. L. Mencken's *American Mercury*. Thompson had become the guest conductor of the Dessoff Choirs in the fall of 1931, and the League of Composers commissioned him to write a work that he could perform with these singers at one of the League's concerts. A search for contemporary verse led him to the bound copies of the *American Mercury* in the New York Public Library. But the idea of a long poem was happily diverted by his discovery of the abundant humor in the "Americana" section of each issue. He decided again to search for a sequence, this time of transcripts of "Americana" which in their contrast would show the diversity of the mores and idiosyncrasies of American life.

The result, the musical *Americana*, is a manual and rich treasurehouse for the study of the challenge of setting to music a great variety of English prose. Consider the textual sources given: 1. *Seattle Post Intelligencer*, 2. *New York Evening Graphic*, 3. *W. C. T. U.*, 4. "Startling Detective Adventures" by a reporter of the *Little Rock Gazette*. 5.

California—Literary intelligence: *Announcing*. Here Thompson establishes his supremacy in the art. For all its satire there is a cherishing of our native foibles and concerns—fundamentalism, spiritualism, temperance, capital punishment, optimism—which is based on a love of our culture. The bite is administered with benevolence. To do this Thompson had just the ingredients and musical predilections for the job. Written over forty years ago, it is astonishing to find how valid these portrayals of Americana still are today. The work would seem to be topical, a period piece, and yet its humor is as fresh as ever. One of the reasons for this is that the composer is using musical allusions which in their innuendoes continue to have the intended impact. "Loveli-lines," the final chorus, provides examples.

The rhythm of the introduction sounds as "corny" now as it did then (Ex. 3).

The quasi-Handelian fugue *a* 4 with a quasi-inverted counterexposition *a* 7, all against a vamp accompaniment, remains a delicious musical joke, which relishes the sense of unquenchable exuberance and high-flying salesmanship so characteristic of our times. Thank heaven that the former is still one of our national traits and that we still can laugh at examples of its excess (Exs. 4a and 4b).

The "blue" note, which Thompson can invoke with equally telling effect in moments ridiculous or sublime, remains one of our musical trade marks. Compare these two phrase endings, respectively from this chorus and the end of Part II of the *Requiem* (Exs. 5a and 5b).

In the early 1930's, the pianist John Powell introduced Thompson to the music of the Sacred Harp Singers. He acquired more than one edition of the *Original Sacred Harp* for study. Most of the tunes were British in origin; they had been brought to New England and gradually taken down the Appalachian Range to the South, where the folk songs were transformed into hymns. Thompson was particularly struck by the role given the tenor of carrying the tune.

A beautiful manifestation of this influence appears in *The Peaceable Kingdom* at the beginning of the fifth chorus (Ex. 6).

That the tenor has the melody is clearly marked, and yet the composer has had more than one occasion to bemoan the fact that a given choir conductor ignored this clear directive. Example 6 shows another lovely feature: the brook, represented by the soprano, has its reflection in the bass, the inversion of the soprano line. The next big phrase (starting at measure 13 of this chorus) suggests the "Fuging Tunes" technique of William Billings, as the melody, now in the alto, is imitated by the soprano.

EXAMPLE 3

In 1935 Thompson's mind was very much taken up with College Music, for he had just completed a study which resulted in a book with this title. He had become an officer of the League of Composers, so it was natural, as the League was considering new kinds of commissions, that he promoted the idea of a work that would be suitable for a

EXAMPLE 4a

given college chorus to introduce by presenting the first performance. The result was that the League commissioned him to write a
work, and the chorus chosen was the combined Harvard Glee Club
and the Radcliffe Choral Society. That summer a painting entitled
"The Peaceable Kingdom" by Edward Hicks, the preaching Quaker
of Pennsylvania, was acquired by the Worcester Art Museum. When
Thompson read of this in the *Boston Evening Transcript*, his curiosity
was aroused. He went to view the painting and became aglow not
only with what he saw but also with the Biblical subject that it por-
trayed. The inscription is a quotation from Isaiah which ends: "for
the earth shall be full of the knowledge of the Lord, as the waters cover
the sea" (11:9). Thompson, like Hicks, who had painted a series of
similar canvases on the subject, was drawn to the theme: the wicked
will be destroyed and the good will go to heaven.

The composer's next move was to read all sixty-six chapters of
Isaiah and copy out those passages that appealed especially. The care
with which he pruned his own selection to arrive at what he has already
described as a sequence based on the unfolding of a dramatic narrative
is reminiscent of Brahms and his preparation of verses for his *German*

EXAMPLE 4b

Requiem. The dream of composing a cycle on sacred texts was realized for the first time. This kind of exacting challenge is for him the most stimulating for the exercise of his craft, and Thompson was to benefit from this experience in the creation of many large works to come: *Mass of the Holy Spirit*, *Requiem*, and the two large works based on Saint Luke, *The Nativity* and *The Passion*.

Another word about the influence of the *Sacred Harp*. The musical language of these hymns was invoked in certain orchestral compositions: specifically, the third movement of his Symphony No. 3 in A minor (see

EXAMPLE 5a

rehearsal number 48, violins) and *A Trip to Nahant*, where "[the couple] approach an old white church where choir rehearsal is going on" (see rehearsal number 51, muted trumpets and trombones). The quote is from the composer's program note.

Of the latter reference he has noted: "The melodies employed are my own. They are characteristic of different kinds of our native tunes, the hymn being patterned after the old hymns in the shape-note manuals."

EXAMPLE 5b

EXAMPLE 6

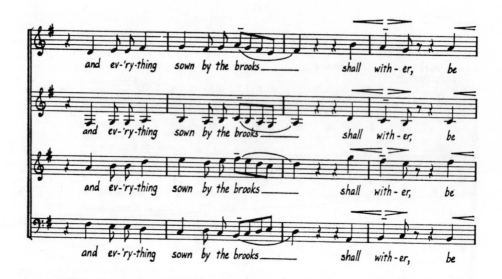

After writing the Suite for Oboe, Clarinet and Viola in 1940, the last movement of which has as its main theme (Ex. 7):

EXAMPLE 7

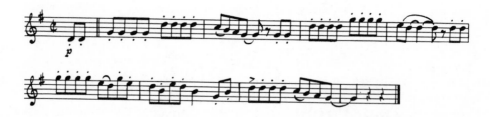

how startled he was to receive from his old friend, Bertrand H. Bronson, the following find (Ex. 8):

EXAMPLE 8

"I hope to shout glory" (G. P. Jackson, *White and Negro Spirituals*, 1943, p. 164)

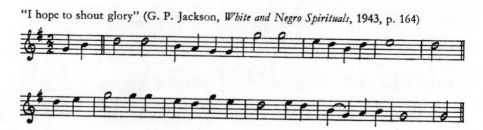

This is not so surprising when one realizes that many of these tunes were Scottish and that Scotland was in the family blood. From his grandfather, Thompson's father learned many of these songs and loved to sing them by the hour while he improvised accompaniments. In this way they were heard, absorbed, and put to new creative uses by a member of the third generation.

The two works that exemplify Thompson's treatment of texts concerned with the development of our country are, of course, the *Ode to the Virginia Voyage* and *The Testament of Freedom*.

The latter was composed in honor of the 200th anniversary of the birth of Thomas Jefferson. The committee in charge of this observance invited Thompson, who was then teaching at the University of Virginia, to write a piece for a professional orchestra. He thought it over and concluded that a composition which honored Jefferson should be a setting of the statesman's words, to be sung by the students of the university that he founded. In 1942 a local newspaper contained a short story about the reconciliation in later life between John Adams and Jefferson, which finally healed the estrangement caused primarily by Adams's appointments just before Jefferson's inauguration. This caught Thompson's eye, and he soon came across Jefferson's letter to Adams, written September 12, 1821 at Monticello, which was to form Part IV of the *Testament*. The incentive was shaped, and, with the help of a colleague in the History Department, he was able to find and to choose other pertinent epoch-making utterances of Jefferson's to round out the text.

No other work has been so closely associated with our national life. The first performance on April 13, 1943, with the University of Virginia Glee Club, Stephen D. Tuttle conducting, the composer at the piano, was broadcast nationally by the Columbia Broadcasting System and recorded by the Office of War Information for rebroadcast to the Armed Forces overseas. The orchestral version of the accompaniment was written shortly afterwards. Of the many performances that followed, the one that meant the most to the composer was that given by Serge Koussevitzky at Carnegie Hall in 1945. A Boston Symphony Orchestra concert had been scheduled, when news came of the death of President Roosevelt. Instead of calling off the concert, Koussevitzky insisted that the concert be given, but open to the public, admission free. The program started with a moment of silence. Then followed the first movement of Shostakovich's Eighth Symphony, the first two movements of Beethoven's *Eroica* Symphony, and *The Testament of Freedom*. At this point Koussevitzky asked for another moment of complete silence and then conducted *The Star Spangled Banner*.

From Virginia again came an invitation of the Commonwealth's

350th Anniversary Commission for a setting of Michael Drayton's *Ode*, to honor the first permanent English settlement in the New World, May, 1607. The text was sent to Thompson in Gstaad, Switzerland, the site of so many of his compositions; he saw the feasibility of its musical setting immediately and accepted the challenge. The focus of this challenge is made clear by the composer's note in the score that this setting "aims to recapture something of the musical spirit of the epoch in which the text was written." The Norfolk Civic Chorus gave the first performance; this writer has heard it sung by secondary school choirs and has prepared it himself with a college chorus for a concert conducted by the composer. Its straightforward character, with its alternation between ceremony, action, and dignified affection, makes it a perfect vehicle for effective performance by any well-formed group of amateur singers.

Our last example of Thompson's *Americana* brings us back to the congeniality that is his in the setting of American verse. When the town of Amherst extended its commission for music to celebrate the 200th anniversary of its incorporation, the suggestion was made to Thompson that he set Frost's *The Gift Outright*. The composer studied the text and decided that its slight overtones of independence would not be suitable for the commemoration of a charter generously extended to the town by George III. The fact that it was to be sung by a combination of local church choirs, however, appealed to him, and he set out on his own to find a sequence of poems that would have shape as a whole, along with internal contrast.

Also, he had in mind the opportunity to put into practice an idea that had occurred to him as an attempt to facilitate a choral preparation which would involve two separate choirs. When a men's chorus from one locality prepares for a joint concert with a women's chorus from another locality, the time for collaboration is often limited. A cycle that contains some sections for men alone and others for women alone reduces the amount of music to be rehearsed when the two choruses finally get together, often on the afternoon of the performance day, for the joint rehearsal. His choice of poems then was influenced by the desire to have an alternation of choral media. The result was seven choruses of which the first, fourth and seventh are for mixed voices, the second and sixth for men's voices, and the third and fifth for women's voices. Furthermore, the first and last choruses take advantage of the fullness of the mixed medium, while the fourth chorus, "The Telephone," shows off the charming contrast in the form of a dialogue that can be made by directly alternating the choruses of the two sexes (an ingenious way of cutting down the problems of a joint rehearsal even further!).

"Choose Something Like a Star," the final chorus, is remarkable in many ways. As in the lovely passage "The morning stars sang together" from the *Requiem* (Part IV, *Molto lento*), the image of a star is created by a sustained pedal for the top voice against chordal movement in the lower three. In the *Frostiana* chorus the lower voices rise in parallel motion. This "theme" is first established by the accompaniment in an ascending scale of quarter notes. The voices in turn rise more slowly with repeated notes and notes of longer rhythmic value. The magic of parallel triadic movement, a staple of Thompson's style, is shown by chords in second inversion (measures 5–8), root position (measures 9–19) and first inversion (measures 20–23). The first section ends at measure 25, at rest on G, the tonic, while the accompaniment reiterates a portion of the faster rising scale as a transition to the modulating second section. In the first five lines Frost has evoked the detachment of the star, and each line's weighty last syllable receives a sustained note by the lower three voices.

The thought in the next twelve lines becomes increasingly restive as the poet demands of the star, "Say something to us we can learn." The musical counterpart is made by another of Thompson's favorite devices, the falling sequence of sevenths over the circle of fifths (Ex. 9).

EXAMPLE 9

This second "theme" enables him to reflect the increasing heat of the text by starting the sequence on successively higher degrees until the crest is reached at measure 49. Here the gathering resignation of the later lines dictates a slow descent, ending with a rhythmic augmentation of the sequential pattern before the cadence is reached at measure 58 on the dominant. Now the music cuts through the division by lines and groups words by meaning and strength of accent.

The final section is a recapitulation in modified form of both the preceding sections. The first musical idea is abbreviated and captures the returning idea of the star's steadfastness (lines 19–21); and the second musical idea, even more abbreviated, even more intense, suggests the frailty of man (lines 22–23). The musical climax and the poem's climax coincide at measure 80, when the rising line of the accompaniment is answered for the first time by the voices rising in equal quarter notes: "We may choose something like a star." The choice has been *suggested* in the text; it has been *affirmed* in music as the voices now experience the directness of the rising line in the accompaniment version of the "theme." A beautiful echo occurs in the tenor's rise in quarter notes (measures 83–84), while the other voices in sustained notes on the tonic chord show that the point of rest is at hand. Against these chorally held tones the accompaniment climbs by steps to high D twice over, ever more softly, the second time compassing the full two octaves from the low D as it had done in the beginning. The last gesture belongs to the accompaniment: a single leap of the two-octave span which ends the chorus, and the work.

Once again a textual passage has been completely analyzed and understood, so that its message may be transmitted and enhanced by musical sound.

The list of choral works given at the end of this volume shows that ever since 1928 Randall Thompson has been creating a continual stream of music written for American choral groups; they may be high school students, college students, or townspeople. As each request for music is fulfilled, usually for a specific occasion, there has been a common element: music that is consistently singable and suited to the text at hand. The composer's craft ensures that in the hearing of this music "the audience has to understand every word." In the last analysis this total accomplishment is what we mean by Randall Thompson's "Americana," for in the writing of this choral music he has performed, with dedication, a great service to his countrymen.

Five Love Songs

REFLECTIONS ON A RECENT WORK

> Some years ago Randall Thompson mentioned to me in the course of a conversation that he was working on a new choral piece. "In what style?" I asked. "In my same old style" was the reply. The question was clumsily put; I had meant to ask about the kind of chorus to be used, or whether the fabric was to be more contrapuntal than chordal .... The answer ... was honest and only in part self-deprecating. For Randall Thompson's large and varied list of compositions ... stand as a monument of calm integrity in a musically turbulent half-century.[1]

The "self-deprecating" reply seems of particular importance to the compiler of the present volume and especially germane to a discussion dealing with Randall Thompson's views on choral composition: it is perhaps significant that his most recent work, *Five Love Songs,* for baritone solo, chorus, and orchestra (in press), offers a wide-angle perspective of the beliefs, teachings, opinions, and discoveries he has set forth in his music for over sixty years. Three of the five movements — *The Light of Stars, The Passenger,* and *Siciliano* — were written in 1918, 1957, and 1966, respectively. Two new choruses — *Two Worlds* and *The Happy Shore* — complete the cycle.

It is doubtful that any composer, much less one working in this "turbulent half-century," could have successfully collated works so disparate in time of origin, and, without pressure or pseudo-artistic devices, welded them into a satisfying whole. But such is the bed-rock, or one might say "atomic structure," of Randall Thompson's choral writing, that, textual and emotional differences laid aside, there is no perception or feeling of stylistic disunity — the new works quote freely from each other and from the earlier pieces, but this is the natural, organic outgrowth of Thompson's compositional method, and in no way an attempt to cover up inevitable changes that must occur in any composer's evolving personal vocabulary.

The compiler's association with Randall Thompson began in 1976. Then a junior at Brandeis University, I met the composer by chance at a Harvard reception in the fall of that year, and, as a result of our conversation, I began to bring him my own compositions for

---

[1] James Haar, "Randall Thompson and the Music of the Past," in *The Choral Music of Randall Thompson* (New York: *American Choral Review,* Vol. XVI, No. 4, October, 1974), p. 7.

criticism on an informal basis. Upon graduating in May, 1978, I began to work as Randall Thompson's secretary and assistant, and continued in that capacity until September, 1979, when I went to the University of Edinburgh. As I reflect on this period, it becomes clear that the most fascinating and vital project we undertook was the composition of *The Happy Shore*, for it was necessary for me to work as Thompson's amanuensis, rapidly taking down dictation, playing back fragments I had transcribed, discussing problems of transitions, and copying pages of sketches to be revised later.

Let me go back a little and examine the origins of the work as a whole. *Five Love Songs* was commissioned by the Rocky Ridge Music Center Foundation early in 1976. When the piece was finished in July, 1978, it had grown from three to five movements, and on the occasion of its première at Estes Park, Colorado, in August, 1978, Thompson had the following to say:

> The most inspiring aspect of my assignment was the spirit from which it grew. From the very beginning of my creative work, it had been my ambition not to wait for an angel with a golden pen to guide my hand. On the contrary, my aesthetic principles resemble those laid down years and years ago; namely, to provide what was needed and requested, and even, if possible, to transcend the terms as they were defined.

When I spoke with Thompson a year later, he had the following to add to this:

> R.T.: The aesthetic principles I referred to were really adopted as the result of various influences during my three years at the American Academy in Rome (1922-25). They owe their origin to the *bottega* system. For example, a painter or an architect in mediaeval society would set up a booth or shop (*bottega*) and take orders or commissions to paint a portrait or design an altar-piece, but always to create something according to the specifations laid down by the patron. These artists worked as one would work for an order. They didn't work only when an inspiration came to them. They worked, and in the process of work they were inspired to transcend the stipulations set forth.

> D.F.U.: In other words, the stipulations laid down by Rocky Ridge were not an obstacle to your own ideas.

> R.T.: No, no. It was merely the jumping-off point. From there I sought to create something richer, better, even more appropriate than they might have conceived of . . . .

> D.F.U.: Three of the pieces in *Five Love Songs* were originally written for different occasions. The first movement, *The Light of Stars*, written when you

were a junior at Harvard, was a competition piece. (It won the Francis Boott Prize in 1918.) The second movement, *The Passenger*, was written for Gerard Souzay, and the fourth movement, *Siciliano*, comes from the music you wrote for Philip H. Rhinelander's *The Gorgonzola.* How did you come to the decision to use these works, and then use two new choruses to complete the cycle?

R.T.: The truth is that Rocky Ridge, commissioning the cycle in memory of a benefactor who had died rather young, did not want an *in memoriam,* but the commemorative spirit is undoubtedly implicit in the various words and music in each of the five movements. The whole cycle of pieces, both the earlier and the later ones, have to do with Love and Death. Each one of the five represents a different way of looking at love: none of them overlap; they rather reflect, from different angles, facets of love.

The first piece, *The Light of Stars,* is a setting of a very early poem by Longfellow. He was trying, idealistically, to sing about love; the poem is a true beginning, which must lead to greater fulfillment. But he is surely a poor, unhappy young man who would

> "give the first watch of night
> to the red planet Mars."

rather than to Aphrodite.

D.F.U.: When you decided to include *The Light of Stars,* you made some revisions, didn't you?

R.T.: Yes, but they were minor ones, corrections of juvenile inconsistencies and such. The text underlay and rhythmic apportionment of text are more maturely dealt with in the published score.

D.F.U.: I recall that when you first showed me *The Light of Stars,* you said, "See, I've written the same sort of music all my life." Now, I don't think this is really true. A thorough analytic study of *The Light of Stars* would show that there are certain hallmarks of your style that are lacking, not even emergent. For the most part, the piece is written in a rather severe style, like much late nineteenth-century choral music, with the significant exception that it betrays an occasional "Monteverdiism" — the work you submitted the following year for the Boott Prize, *The Last Invocation,* shows even more clearly, I think, the extent of Monteverdi's influence on the works you wrote before your stay in Rome. As a competition piece, *The Light of Stars* tries to include something of everything — cross-relations, somewhat Franckesque chromaticism, several kinds of canon, etc. But it *is* remarkably poetic and expressive. I'm sure the following passage was the height of musical sensuality at Harvard in 1918 (Ex. 3):

R.T.: I think that this is so!

D.F.U.: What about *The Passenger?*

EXAMPLE 3

R.T.: This comes next, and represents a great advance in terms of the emotional content of the text over the first piece. Here, in a poem written on the author's ninetieth birthday, is a real sense of achievement. It's not tearful, but it's not a rollicking love song, either. I included it because I felt it provided the proper change of mood and also provided one of the two solos that separate the three choruses of the entire cycle.

D.F.U.: The next piece, *Two Worlds*, written in 1977, has a text obviously full of meaning for you . . . .

R.T.: Yes, this is true. It is sometimes called *Old Age*, but I have called it *Two Worlds* because it is so packed with the fullness of life. The old world and the new are, each in its own way, full of meaning and devotion. I composed this first, however, and so it contains no musically thematic references to the other pieces.

D.F.U.: The fourth movement, *Siciliano*, is uncomplicated . . . .

R.T.: (cutting in) Yes, yes, but it too is based on antitheses; e.g.,

> In summer blue and gold;
> in winter black and cold;
>
> In summer a dancing madness;
> in autumn staring sadness;
>
> In summer silver bright;
> in winter dark as night.[2]

[2] Quoted from Philip H. Rhinelander, *The Gorgonzola; Tavern Club Christmas Play*, Boston, 1966.

D.F.U.: The final chorus, *The Happy Shore,* is the most interesting in many respects. This may be because of my personal involvement in it, but it has certain things about it that make it unique. First, it is your most recent work. Secondly, and more important, it is largely constructed out of thematic material from *The Passenger* and *Two Worlds.* To what extent was this an attempt to create a cyclic effect, and to what extent a natural outgrowth of the compositional process?

R.T.: That's a hard question to answer. I think that there is no doubt but that a sonnet is a very difficult thing to set, and I approached that with fear and trembling because I didn't know whether I would be able to do it well and at the same time imbue it with the right emotional significance. As a matter of fact, I was encouraged in doing so by studying the sonnet settings of Monteverdi, and the greatest that I know of is the bipartite *Hor che'l ciel e la terra,* for six-part chorus and two violins. Setting a sonnet requires a special flexibility — there is no corresponding form in music to match the sonnet's metrical structure. In utilizing fragments or motifs from *The Passenger* and *Two Worlds,* I was trying to unify the very different aspects of each of the *Five Love Songs.* Quoting motifs and themes in the last movement gave a certain cyclic coherence to the total work so that it is not just a set of unrelated choruses. It became, in essence, one extended piece, and I would say that I deliberately quoted from earlier movements. There are very explicit relationships, as you well know, and Spenser's *The Happy Shore* is now thematically and emotionally linked with *The Passenger* and *Two Worlds . . . .*

In asking Randall Thompson about a work process that I knew through close involvement from its earliest stages, I was, perhaps, not playing fair. *The Happy Shore,* though a work that can be perfectly well performed apart from the entire cycle, does unify the *Five Love Songs,* and it provides a climax of great intensity when the cycle is performed as a whole. *The Happy Shore* opens in somber G minor (Ex. 4):

EXAMPLE 4

The original motif, from *The Passenger,* runs thus:

EXAMPLE 5

At bar 10, the chorus enters with a tune borrowed from *Two Worlds:*

EXAMPLE 6

Two Worlds

EXAMPLE 7

The Happy Shore

Each line of the sonnet is given a similar, chorale-like treatment, coming to a half-cadence at the close of the phrase, and interrupted by a stabilizing passage for strings over a pedal-point. The exception occurs at bar 36 with the words "Fair soil it seems from far and fraught with store/of all that dear and dainty is alive," where the sopranos soar over the chorus, and the music (derived from a similar passage at measure 33 of *Two Worlds*) descends over a sequence of seventh chords, one of the composer's favorite devices (Ex. 8):

EXAMPLE 8

At bar 55, the passage is repeated in inversion, a minor third lower at the words "Remembrance of all pains which him oppress'd." The final couplet, so important to the composer, is tellingly marked *con solazione,* and the chorus, on an octave G, fades over the strings that begin again to quote the *Passenger* "Alleluia" in triads whose parallel motion is offset by voice crossings.

But the first violin rises on an arpeggio, over another reference (derived from *The Passenger*), at last in serene G major, the composer's favorite key (Ex. 9):

EXAMPLE 9

Thompson's solution to the mentioned "sonnet problem" besetting the composer is successful and unique. Many other sonnet settings of our day (Britten's *Sonnets of Michelangelo* and Halsey Stevens's *Like as the culver on the barèd bough* — another setting of a sonnet from Edmund Spenser's *Amoretti,* from which *The Happy Shore* is taken) are rhapsodic and *durchkomponiert.* Quite apart from that, Thompson's setting is reminiscent of some extended chorale settings of Bach's; e.g., the final chorus, "O grosser Gott von Treu'," in Cantata 46, where a moderately elaborated chorale melody is interrupted at each cadence by a descending scale passage for two recorder parts.

Finally, it is interesting to note here the other passage work in which Thompson utilizes the "Alleluia" from *The Passenger;* namely, the final section of his *Requiem.*[3] Here the setting is for double chorus. Chorus II has just finished an expressive Amen setting, when, at bar 22, Chorus I enters *ppp come da lontano* — a striking effect (Ex. 10):

It is rather too obvious to say that the word "Alleluia" is especially dear to the heart of Randall Thompson (witness his comments in the second and third essays of this issue), but certainly his use of the melody he originally devised over twenty years ago in *The Passenger* had been carefully designed, and it provides a subtle thread of continuity through his varied *oeuvre.*

I have commented at some length on some of Thompson's compositional techniques and his approach to the craft of composition, using a recent work for exemplification. But the purely artistic issue seemed an equally vital, if somewhat more elusive, aspect for the commentator to approach on his own:

[3] For the composer's own assessment, see *American Choral Review,* Vol. XVI, No. 4, p. 31.

EXAMPLE 10

D.F.U.: It has been said before, to the point of exaggeration, that you have never written anything that was not first commissioned. I think, more than anything else, this reflects on what you earlier referred to as "principles laid down years ago." One hears many composers say, "I wrote such and such a piece to explore this form, or that medium, etc." Does that sort of impetus ever influence the commissions you accept? For example, if you were casting about for a text for a large choral work, would you turn down a commission for a symphony?

R.T.: Well, I think that brings us to the question of Classic versus Romantic attitudes towards music and art in general. There are composers (or painters or sculptors, for that matter) who simply won't accept commissions — unless they're heaven-sent, of course! They are the people who write "Romantic" music, and we are still immersed in that. So much contemporary music is totally devoid of spontaneity, or of an intent to delight a particular audience. Such composers tend to write purely for self-expression.

D.F.U.: Wouldn't that be more accurately called "Expressionism"? Expressionism is commonly supposed to repudiate Romantic ideals. Do you feel that somehow those two terms define the style, whereas the intent and spirit of Expressionism in music remains as much a child of the nineteenth century as the music *of* the nineteenth century?

R.T.: I would call it a "nineteenth-century-twentieth-century style." The laboring for self-expression is just what's wrong with what many composers are doing. If, to return to our discussion, you take my *Five Love Songs,* you'll see that it begins on quite a sad note. In *The Light of Stars* the young Longfellow is an unrequited lover, bitter and barren. *The Passenger* is a song of parting and death, but it is anything but downcast. *Two Worlds* is a different interpretation of death, but it is not sad, it is not *triste,* or tragic, or crying out in pain. *The Happy Shore* is a consummate expression of the whole complex of ideas. I was so delighted to conclude with it because of the poignant beauty of the last couplet:

> All pains are nothing in respect of this,
> All sorrows short that gain eternal bliss.

which undoubtedly refers to death. I didn't try to write a "melodrama" that would make people cry, but I was bound to write a memorial. I wrote one that could confront sadness without being grief-stricken, and loss without gloom. That is what I mean when I speak of Classicism in music. I think that in all good music, all good art, the best things transcend tears and express something that is built out of sadnesss, but rises through spiritual elevation to truth, beauty, and love.

D.F.U.: Would you say that this is something intrinsically bound up with Classical art?

R.T.: Yes, rather than the bathos and sentimentality so dear to the Romantics.

D.F.U.: It would seem that the qualities you define as Classical are, in Schopenhauerian terms, Transcendent, or "real," whereas the Romantic is Immanent, or "unreal."

R.T.: Exactly. My settings of Horace, for example, are one manifestation of the way Classicism, as I have defined it, becomes "real," is woven into my musical fiber and expression. Those pieces were a response to my enthusiasm for Classical art. Obviously, emotional aridity and imbalance will produce nothing but weak creative work, and it seems to me that composers who write only for self-expression do so because their emotions are fettered to the Romantic past and not guided by the Classical . . . .

It is readily apparent that Thompson's "Classical" attitude is at the bottom of all his creative work; it is deeply ingrained in his artistic subconscious. In the case of such a composer, so well known and loved by musicians (especially singers) throughout the world, it is a bit strange to find that, unlike most composers of his experience, he has only recently been able to devote all of his energies to composition. From 1927 until his retirement in 1965 he was on the teaching faculties of Wellesley, Berkeley, Curtis, University of Virginia, Princeton, and Harvard, and found a good deal of his time for writing in the interstices of his teaching duties, or while on vacation at his chalet in Gstaad. Some of his music was not only written on commission but also "at the point of a gun," as he has described Koussevitsky's request for a choral work, which (a few days later) turned out to be *The Last Words of David*. The *Alleluia* was written only a few days prior to the opening of the Berkshire Music Center at Tanglewood. In a letter to his old friend and classmate Leopold D. Mannes, he confessed that he had chosen the word "Alleluia" because it greatly reduced the problem of having to teach, in one rehearsal, proper diction to a chorus that had never sung together before.

It is not for nothing that Thompson is everywhere referred to as "composer and educator." He is the first to admit that much of the stimulus for his own creative work has lain in teaching. The craftsman, in Classical art, needs his apprentices, his students, to remind him that one never really ceases to be a student; that being a composer, an artist, is a process of perpetual maturing. In a world rife with the hysteric search for self-expression, it is sad, though not surprising, that few composers have understood the value of Thompson's classicism, its honesty, and its philosophical reality. James Haar said in the essay referred to at the beginning of this article that for Thompson ". . . the *Angst* of the modern composer-academic has not been an issue." This *Angst* is the bequest of the past century, in whose unsettled debts we are now immersed. But for the choral singer, the conductor, and all who have experienced the "songs of his passion,"[4] Randall Thompson has created his own legacy, a legacy that is personal for the sake of sharing his experience with others and that will remain of ineffable quality.

All musical examples taken from the works of Randall Thompson are reproduced with the kind permission of E.C. Schirmer Music Company.

[4]Quoted from Robert Louis Stevenson, "Bright is the ring of words," in *Songs of Travel*, 1894.

List of Choral Works by Randall Thompson

Compiled by ELLIOT FORBES

SECULAR WORKS	Date	First performance
Odes of Horace (Quintus Horatius Flaccus)	1924	Rome
Quis multa gracilis te (*Odes* I, 5)		May 16, 1925
TTBB *a cappella*		Choir of San
Vitas hinnuleo me similis, Chloë (I, 23)		Salvatore in Lauro
SATB *a cappella*		
O Venus, regina Cnidi Paphique (I, 30)		
SSATTBB with piano or chamber orchestra		
O fons Bandusiae, splendidior vitro (III, 13)		
SSATBB *a cappella*		
Montium custos nemorumque, Virgo (III, 22)		
SATB *a cappella*		
Rosemary (Stephen Vincent Benét)	1929	New York, N.Y.
SSAA *a cappella*		December 18, 1930
1. Chemical Analysis		Women's Univer-
2. A Sad Song		sity Glee Club
3. A Nonsense Song		
4. To Rosemary on the methods by which she might become an angel		
Americana (from *The American Mercury*)	1932	New York, N.Y.
SATB with piano or orchestra		April 4, 1932
Commissioned by the League of Composers		A Cappella Singers
1. May Every Tongue		
2. The Staff Necromancer		
3. God's Bottles (SSAA)		
4. The Sublime Process of Law Enforcement		
5. Loveli-lines		
Tarantella (Hilaire Belloc)	1937	New Haven, Conn.
TTBB with piano or orchestra		November 12, 1937
		Yale Glee Club

SECULAR WORKS	Date	First performance
Solomon and Balkis (Rudyard Kipling) 　Opera for five soloists, SA chorus and orchestra 　Commissioned by the League of Composers 　　and the Columbia Broadcasting System	1942	New York, N.Y. March 29, 1942 Columbia Broadcasting System; Columbia Concert Orchestra Staged: Cambridge, Mass. April 14, 1942 Harvard's Lowell House Musical Society
The Testament of Freedom (Thomas Jefferson) 　TTBB with piano, orchestra, or band 　In honor of the 200th Anniversary of the 　Birth of Thomas Jefferson	1943	Charlottesville, Va. April 13, 1943 University of Virginia Glee Club With orchestra: Boston, Mass. April 6, 1945 Boston Symphony Orchestra
Odes of Horace 　Felices ter (I, 13) 　　SATB *a cappella* 　For Archibald T. Davison	1953	
Ode to the Virginian Voyage (Michael Drayton) 　SATB with orchestra 　In honor of the first permanent English 　Settlement in the New World, May, 1607	1956–57	Williamsburg, Va. April 1, 1957 Norfolk Symphony Orchestra and Civic Chorus and William and Mary College Choir
Frostiana (Robert Frost) 　Seven Country Songs with piano or orchestra 　For the 200th Anniversary of the Charter of the 　Town of Amherst, Massachusetts 　1. The Road Not Taken, SATB 　2. The Pasture, TBB 　3. Come In, SAA 　4. The Telephone, SAA/TTBB 　5. A Girl's Garden, SAA	1959	Amherst, Mass. October 18, 1959 With orchestra: Cambridge, Mass. April 23, 1965 Harvard Glee Club, Radcliffe Choral Society and Harvard-Radcliffe Orchestra

SECULAR WORKS	Date	First performance

6. Stopping by Woods on a Snowy Evening,
   TBB

7. Choose Something Like a Star, SATB
   (Also arranged for women's voices)

	Date	First performance
Fare Well (Walter De La Mare) SATB *a cappella*	1973	Merrick, N.Y. March 4, 1973 Combined Calhoun, Kennedy, and Mepham High School Choirs

SACRED WORKS	Date	First performance
Two Amens SATB *a cappella*	1927	St. Luke's Church Montclair, N.J. February 26, 1927
Pueri Hebraeorum SSAA/SSAA *a cappella*	1928	Wellesley, Mass. February 5, 1928 Wellesley College Choir

	Date	First performance
The Peaceable Kingdom (Isaiah) SATB *a cappella* Commissioned by the League of Composers	1936	Cambridge, Mass. March 3, 1936 Harvard Glee Club and Radcliffe Choral Society

1. Say ye to the righteous
2. Woe unto them
3. The noise of a multitude
4. Howl ye, SATB/SATB
5. The paper reeds by the brooks
6. Recit.: But these are they that forsake the
        Lord
        For ye shall go out with joy, SATB/
        SATB
7. Have ye not known?
8. Ye shall have a song, SSAA/TTBB

	Date	First performance
Alleluia SATB *a cappella* (Also arranged for women's voices and for men's voices) For the first Opening Exercises of the Berkshire Music Center	1940	Lenox, Mass. July 8, 1940 Berkshire Festival Chorus

Sacred Works	Date	First performance

The Last Words of David
SATB with piano, orchestra, or band
(Also arranged for men's voices)
Commissioned by the Boston Symphony
Orchestra in honor of the 25th Anniversary of
the Directorship of Serge Koussevitzky

1949

Lenox, Mass.
August 12, 1949

Berkshire Music
Center Student
Body and Boston
Symphony
Orchestra

Mass of the Holy Spirit
Kyrie, SATB with SAT soli *a cappella*
Gloria, SATB and SSAA/TTBB
Credo, SATB
Sanctus, SAATTBB
Benedictus, SATB
Hosanna, SATB
Agnus Dei, SATB
To the Choir of St. Stephen's Church,
Providence, Rhode Island

1955–56

Cambridge, Mass.
March 22, 1957
Harvard Glee Club
and Radcliffe
Choral Society

Requiem
SATB/SATB *a cappella*
Commissioned by the University of California for
the dedication of its new music buildings

1957–58

Berkeley, Calif.
May 22, 1958
University of
California Chorus

Glory to God in the Highest (Luke)
SATB *a cappella*

1958

Stanford, Calif.
Stanford University
Summer School
Chorus

The Gate of Heaven
SSAA *a cappella*
(Also arranged for mixed voices and for
men's voices)
For the dedication of the DuPont Chapel,
Hollins College, Virginia

1959

Hollins College, Va.
February 22, 1959
Hollins College
Choir

The Nativity According to Saint Luke
A Musical Drama in Seven Scenes
Twelve Soloists, SATB, children's choir and
chamber orchestra
(Nowel [Scene VI] also arranged for women's
voices and for men's voices)
For the 200th Anniversary of the Dedication
of Christ Church, Cambridge, Massachusetts

1961

Cambridge, Mass.
December 13, 1961
Christ Church Choir
with orchestra

Sacred Works	Date	First performance
The Lord is my shepherd SSAA and piano or organ (Also arranged for mixed voices)	1962	New York, N.Y. May 1, 1964 Chapin School Choral Club
The Best of Rooms (Robert Herrick) SATB *a cappella*	1963	Evanston, Ill. April 7, 1963 Northwestern University Chorus
A Feast of Praise SATB with brass choir and harp or piano Commissioned by the Department of Music, Stanford University	1963	Stanford, Calif. August 11, 1963 Stanford University Summer Chorus
Hymn: *Thy Book Falls Open, Lord* (David McCord) For the Harvard University Hymn Book An accompaniment for band was made by the composer for use at Harvard Commencement, 1964	1964	
The Passion according to Saint Luke An Oratorio in Ten Scenes Soloists and SATB with orchestra For the 150th Anniversary of the Founding of the Handel and Haydn Society	1964–65	Boston, Mass. March 28, 1965 Handel and Haydn Society and Cambridge Festival Orchestra
A Psalm of Thanksgiving SATB and children's chorus with orchestra, piano, or organ	1967	Boston, Mass. November 15, 1967 New England Conservatory Choruses and Symphony Orchestra
The Eternal Dove (Joseph Beaumont) SATB *a cappella* For G. Wallace Woodworth	1968	Cambridge, Mass. May 17, 1970 Harvard University Choir
The Place of the Blest (Robert Herrick and Richard Wilbur) SSAA with piano or chamber orchestra In honor of the 50th Anniversary of the Founding of Saint Thomas Choir School	1969	New York, N.Y. March 2, 1969 St. Thomas Church Boys Choir

SACRED WORKS	Date	First performance
Two Herbert Settings (George Herbert)		New York, N.Y.
1. Bitter-sweet, SATB *a cappella*	1970	October 25, 1970
		Church of the Incarnation Choir
2. Antiphon, SATB *a cappella*	1971	—
The Mirror of St. Anne (Isaac Watts)	1972	
SATB/SATB		
An antiphonal setting in Inverse Contrary Imitation		
(Original version of devotional orchestral interlude in Part IV of *Ode to the Virginian Voyage*)		
A Hymn for Scholars and Pupils (George Wither)	1973	
Version 1 for treble voices and chamber orchestra		Washington, Conn. June 8, 1973
Version 2 for SATB, organ and chamber orchestra (with double bass and trombone parts added)		Raleigh, N.C. November 11, 1973

ADDENDUM

	Date	First performance
The Lark in the Morn SATB, *a cappella*	1938	Berkeley, Calif. December 2, 1938 University of California Chorus
Now I lay me down to sleep SSA, *a cappella*	1947	In class: Princeton University May 8, 1947 Princeton, New Jersey
A Concord Cantáta	1975	Concord, Mass.
SATB and orchestra		May 2, 1975
1. The Ballad of the Bridge (Hale)		Concord Chorus with Nashua Symphony
2. Inscription (French)		
3. The Gift Outright (Frost)		

ADDENDUM (cont'd)	Date	First performance
Five Love Songs	1978	Estes Park, Colo.
Baritone solo, SATB, piano and strings		August 6, 1978
Commissioned by the Rocky Ridge Music Center as a bequest in memory of Tell Ertl.		Rocky Ridge Chorale and Orchestra

1. The Light of Stars
   SATB *a cappella*

2. The Passenger, baritone solo and piano
   (strings *ad lib.*)

3. Two Worlds, SATB and piano (strings
   ad lib.)

4. Siciliano (Love is like a wind upon the
   water), baritone solo and piano (strings *ad
   lib.*)

5. The Happy Shore
   SATB, piano or strings

BIBLIOGRAPHY

Porter, Quincy. "American Composers, XVIII, Randall Thompson," in *Modern Music*, XIX (1942), pp. 237-42. Includes list of works composed 1919-42.

Forbes, Elliot. "The Music of Randall Thompson," in *The Musical Quarterly*, XXXV (1949), pp. 1-25. Includes list of works composed 1922-43.

See also catalogue of E. C. Schirmer Music Company, 112 South Street, Boston, MA.

Index of Choral Works